# THE WORDS OF JESUS

# THE WORDS OF JESUS

**AXIOS PRESS**

Arlington, Virginia

**Axios Press, Inc.**
1110 N. Glebe Road, Suite 1100
Arlington, VA 22201-4795

Printed in the United States of America
2000 99 98     5 4 3 2 1st edition

Library of Congress Catalog Card Number: 98-70605
ISBN 0-9661908-2-3

The cover shows the miniature that appears on folio 198 verso of
Ludolphus De Saxonia, *Vita Christi*, Bruges, 1485, illuminated by the
Master of Edward IV for Johann II von Oettingen. Here Christ, sitting
on the Mount of Olives, foretells the destruction of the Temple, with
the signs that shall come before it and the last judgment (Matthew 24).
Axios Press, Inc., is indebted to the Pierpont Morgan Library for its
generous assistance in providing the miniature.

All quotations of scripture are taken from the Authorized
King James Version of the Bible.

# CONTENTS

# ACKNOWLEDGMENTS

The editor is especially indebted to Carol Anschuetz and Craig Smith for their invaluable guidance and assistance with the project; to Kathleen Chabra for her assistance in editing Part I; and to Stephanie Pasha for her meticulous proofreading of the text.

# EDITOR'S NOTE

The canonical gospels, Matthew, Mark, Luke and John, provide not only Jesus' words, but also his actions, the context within which the words are spoken. Why then extract Jesus' words alone?

There are three principal reasons for doing so. The first reason is that isolating his words makes them even more immediate and unmistakable. When we are confronted directly with a saying, we cannot glide over it as we follow the general contour of the story. A second reason is that the words taken alone are compact, 44,382 in all; so we can either linger over them and study them intently or read them all in one sitting. A third reason is that extracting words permits us to compare similar teachings from different gospels more directly than we can by using a standard concordance.

This collection of the words of Jesus is in some sense an experiment. The complete words have never been extracted and published alone, to the best of our knowledge, so we will have to see if readers find it useful. The layout is as follows. Part I provides a selection of particularly well known sayings from all four gospels presented as a kind of dramatic monologue. It is as if Jesus were speaking directly to each of us. Part II presents additional sayings that are not quite so often quoted but still seem very important. Some of these slightly less well known sayings may be initially startling, as in Matthew, chapter 10, verse 34 ("I came not to send peace, but a sword"), by which Jesus presumably means that his teachings are inherently controversial and demanding and that they may even divide family members from one another.

Part III provides all of Jesus' words from all the gospels in the order in which they appear to have been spoken. Thus it repeats material covered in Parts I and II but fills in the remainder of Jesus' words. It is in part a chronology and, like all chronologies, inevitably involves some guesswork, since the gospels are not always concerned with the exact sequence of events, and it is not always clear where an episode presented in only one gospel might have fit into another. However, Part III is more than a chronology because it not only lists events but actually quotes the full text of the words spoken at each point in time. To the best of our knowledge, this has also never been attempted before.

The advantage of gathering the words from all four gospels in Part III in more or less chronological order is that it follows the story of Jesus' life more closely than a random collection of sayings, and it enables us to group together different gospel accounts of the same or similar sayings so that we can readily compare them. In cases where Jesus' words are the same or similar from gospel to gospel and where they seem to be spoken at more or less the same time to the same person or persons, we have simply presented the different gospel versions one after another. Where Jesus' words are similar from gospel to gospel but seem to be spoken at a different time or to a different person or persons, we have placed the heading "Related Sayings" above the passages in question. Whether the similar sayings are contextually identical or contextually different, the objective of grouping them in Part III is to help us reflect on their meaning, not to compare them word for word as a biblical scholar might.

Finally and importantly, this book is in no sense meant to substitute for the gospels themselves. The editor assumes that the words of Jesus will lead readers back to the gospels themselves again and again to place passages in exact context.

*Hunter Lewis*

# PART I

# SELECTED SAYINGS

These are the words which I spake unto you, while    Lk 24:44
I was yet with you...

## Epiphany

Come unto me, all ye that labour and are heavy    Mt 11:28
laden, and I will give you rest.

Take my yoke upon you, and learn of me; for I am    29
meek and lowly in heart: and ye shall find rest unto
your souls.

For my yoke is easy, and my burden is light.    30

Whosoever drinketh of...water shall thirst again:    Jn 4:13

But whosoever drinketh of the water that I shall    14
give him shall never thirst;...the water that I shall
give him shall be in him a well of water springing
up into everlasting life.

Let not your heart be troubled: ye believe in God,    Jn 14: 1
believe also in me.

In my Father's house are many mansions: if it were    2
not so, I would have told you. I go to prepare a
place for you.

And if I go and prepare a place for you, I will come    3
again, and receive you unto myself; that where I
am, there ye may be also.

If any man will come after me, let him deny him-    Mt 16:24
self, and take up his cross, and follow me.

For whosoever will save his life shall lose it: and whosoever will lose his life for my sake shall find it.

25

For what is a man profited, if he shall gain the whole world, and lose his own soul? or what shall a man give in exchange for his soul?

26

Yet a little while am I with you, and then I go unto him that sent me.

Jn 7:33

Behold my hands and my feet, that it is I myself: handle me, and see; for a spirit hath not flesh and bones, as ye see me have.

Lk 24:39

Yet a little while is the light with you. Walk while ye have the light, lest darkness come upon you: for he that walketh in darkness knoweth not whither he goeth.

Jn 12:35

While ye have light, believe in the light, that ye may be the children of light.

36

[For the] Son of man shall come in his glory, and all the holy angels with him...[to] sit upon the throne of his glory:

Mt 25:31

And before him shall be gathered all nations: and he shall separate them one from another....

32

[The unrighteous] shall go away into everlasting punishment: but the righteous into life eternal.

46

## The Moral Life

Think not that I am come to destroy the law, or the prophets: I am not come to destroy, but to fulfil.   Mt 5:17

Thou shalt love the Lord thy God with all thy heart, and with all thy soul, and with all thy mind.   Mt 22:37

This is the first and great commandment.   38

And the second is like unto it, Thou shalt love thy neighbor as thyself.   39

On these two commandments hang all the law and the prophets.   40

Ye have heard that it hath been said, An eye for an eye, and a tooth for a tooth:   Mt 5:38

But I say unto you, That ye resist not evil: but whosoever shall smite thee on thy right cheek, turn to him the other also.   39

And if any man will sue thee at the law, and take away thy coat, let him have thy cloke also.   40

And whosoever shall compel thee to go a mile, go with him twain.   41

Give to him that asketh thee, and from him that would borrow of thee turn not thou away.   42

Take heed to yourselves: If thy brother trespass against thee, rebuke him; and if he repent, forgive him.   Lk 17: 3

And if he trespass against thee seven times in a day, and seven times in a day turn again to thee, saying, I repent; thou shalt forgive him.   4

Ye have [also] heard that it hath been said, Thou shalt love thy neighbour, and hate thine enemy.

Mt 5:43

But I say unto you, Love your enemies, bless them that curse you, do good to them that hate you, and pray for them which despitefully use you, and persecute you.

44

A certain man went down from Jerusalem to Jericho, and fell among thieves, which stripped him of his raiment, and wounded him, and departed, leaving him half dead.

Lk 10:30

And by chance there came down a certain priest that way: and when he saw him, he passed by on the other side.

31

And likewise a Levite, when he was at the place, came and looked on him, and passed by on the other side.

32

But a certain Samaritan, as he journeyed, came where he was: and when he saw him, he had compassion on him.

33

And went to him, and bound up his wounds, pouring in oil and wine, and set him on his own beast, and brought him to an inn, and took care of him.

34

And on the morrow when he departed, he took out two pence, and gave them to the host, and said unto him, Take care of him; and whatsoever thou spendest more, when I come again, I will repay thee.

35

[So] if ye love them which love you, what reward have ye? do not even the publicans the same?

Mt 5:46

And if ye salute your brethren only, what do ye more than others? do not even the publicans so? 47

Ye have [also] heard that it was said by them of old time, Thou shall not kill; and whosoever shall kill shall be in danger of the judgment: Mt 5:21

But I say unto you, That whosoever is angry with his brother without a cause shall be in danger of the judgment:...but whosoever shall say, Thou fool, shall be in danger of hell fire. 22

Ye have heard that it was said by them of old time, Thou shalt not commit adultery: 27

But I say unto you, That whosoever looketh on a woman to lust after her hath committed adultery with her already in his heart. 28

And if thy right eye offend thee, pluck it out, and cast it from thee: for it is profitable for thee that one of thy members should perish, and not that thy whole body should be cast into hell. 29

It hath [also] been said, Whosoever shall put away his wife, let him give her a writing of divorcement: 31

But I say unto you, That whosoever shall put away his wife, saving for the cause of fornication, causeth her to commit adultery: and whosoever shall marry her that is divorced committeth adultery. 32

Again, ye have heard that it hath been said by them of old time, Thou shalt not forswear thyself, but shalt perform unto the Lord thine oaths: 33

But I say unto you, Swear not at all; neither by heaven; for it is God's throne: 34

Nor by the earth; for it is his footstool: neither by    35
Jerusalem; for it is the city of the great King.

But let your communication be, Yea, yea; Nay,    37
nay: for whatsoever is more than these cometh of
evil.

[A]ll things whatsoever ye would that men should    Mt 7:12
do to you, do ye even so to them: for this is the law
and the prophets.

[And] judge not, that ye be not judged.    1

For with what judgment ye judge, ye shall be judged:    2
and with what measure ye mete, it shall be measured to you again.

And why beholdest thou the mote that is in thy    3
brother's eye, but considerest not the beam that is
in thine own eye?

Thou hypocrite, first cast out the beam out of thine    5
own eye; and then shalt thou see clearly to cast out
the mote out of thy brother's eye.

If any man desire to be first, the same shall be last    Mk 9:35
of all, and servant of all.

When thou art bidden of any man to a wedding,    Lk 14: 8
sit not down in the highest room....

But when thou art bidden, go and sit down in the    10
lowest room; that when he that bade thee cometh,
he may say unto thee, Friend, go up higher....

For whosoever exalteth himself shall be abased; and    11
he that humbleth himself shall be exalted.

When thou makest a dinner or a supper, call not    Lk 14:12
thy friends, nor thy brethren, neither thy kinsmen,

nor thy rich neighbours; lest they also bid thee again, and a recompence be made thee.

But when thou makest a feast, call the poor, the maimed, the lame, the blind:　13

And thou shalt be blessed: for they cannot recompense thee: for thou shalt be recompensed at the resurrection of the just.　14

[Also] take heed, and beware of covetousness: for a man's life consisteth not in the abundance of things which he possesseth.　Lk 12:15

The ground of a certain rich man brought forth plentifully:　Lk 12:16

And he thought within himself, saying, What shall I do, because I have no room where to bestow my fruits?　17

And he said, This will I do: I will pull down my barns, and build greater; and there will I bestow all my fruits and my goods.　18

And I will say to my soul, Soul, thou hast much goods laid up for many years; take thine ease, eat, drink, and be merry.　19

But God said unto him, Thou fool, this night thy soul shall be required of thee: then whose shall those things be, which thou hast provided?　20

There was [another] rich man, which was clothed in purple and fine linen, and fared sumptuously every day:　Lk 16:19

And there was a certain beggar named Lazarus, which was laid at his gate, full of sores,　20

And desiring to be fed with the crumbs which fell from the rich man's table: moreover the dogs came and licked his sores.　21

And it came to pass, that the beggar died, and was carried by the angels into Abraham's bosom: the rich man also died, and was buried;  22

And in hell he lift up his eyes, being in torments, and seeth Abraham afar off, and Lazarus in his bosom.  23

And he cried and said, Father Abraham, have mercy on me, and send Lazarus, that he may dip the tip of his finger in water, and cool my tongue; for I am tormented in this flame.  24

But Abraham said, Son, remember that thou in thy lifetime receivedst thy good things, and likewise Lazarus evil things: but now he is comforted, and thou art tormented.  25

[Therefore] lay not up for yourselves treasures upon earth, where moth and rust doth corrupt, and where thieves break through and steal:  Mt 6:19

But lay up for yourselves treasures in heaven, where neither moth nor rust doth corrupt, and where thieves do not break through nor steal:  20

For where your treasure is, there will your heart be also.  21

Verily I say unto you, That a rich man shall hardly enter into the kingdom of heaven.  Mt 19:23

And again I say unto you, It is easier for a camel to go through the eye of a needle, than for a rich man to enter into the kingdom of God.  24

(With men this is impossible; but with God all things are possible.)  26

[Moreover] I say unto you, Take no thought for your life, what ye shall eat, or what ye shall drink;  Mt 6:25

nor yet for your body, what ye shall put on. Is not the life more than meat, and the body than raiment?

Behold the fowls of the air: for they sow not, neither do they reap, nor gather into barns; yet your heavenly Father feedeth them. Are ye not much better than they? 26

Which of you by taking thought can add one cubit unto his stature? 27

And why take ye thought for raiment? Consider the lilies of the field, how they grow; they toil not, neither do they spin: 28

And yet I say unto you, That even Solomon in all his glory was not arrayed like one of these. 29

Wherefore, if God so clothe the grass of the field, which to day is, and to morrow is cast into the oven, shall he not much more clothe you, O ye of little faith? 30

Therefore take no thought, saying, What shall we eat? or, What shall we drink? or, Wherewithal shall we be clothed? 31

(For after all these things do the Gentiles seek:) for your heavenly Father knoweth that ye have need of all these things. 32

But seek ye first the kingdom of God, and his righteousness; and all these things shall be added unto you. 33

Take therefore no thought for the morrow: for the morrow shall take thought for the things of itself. Sufficient unto the day is the evil thereof. 34

Beware ye [also] of the leaven of the Pharisees, which is hypocrisy. Lk 12: 1

For there is nothing covered, that shall not be revealed; neither hid, that shall not be known.

2

Therefore whatsoever ye have spoken in darkness shall be heard in the light; and that which ye have spoken in the ear in closets shall be proclaimed upon the housetops.

3

Two men went up into the temple to pray; the one a Pharisee, and the other a publican.

Lk 18:10

The Pharisee stood and prayed thus with himself, God, I thank thee, that I am not as other men are, extortioners, unjust, adulterers, or even as this publican.

11

I fast twice in the week, I give tithes of all that I possess.

12

And the publican, standing afar off, would not lift up so much as his eyes unto heaven, but smote upon his breast, saying, God be merciful to me a sinner.

13

I tell you, this man went down to his house justified rather than the other: for every one that exalteth himself shall be abased; and he that humbleth himself shall be exalted.

14

[Therefore] take heed that ye do not your alms before men, to be seen of them: otherwise ye have no reward of your Father which is in heaven.

Mt 6: 1

[W]hen thou doest thine alms, do not sound a trumpet before thee, as the hypocrites do in the synagogues and in the streets, that they may have glory of men. Verily I say unto you, They have their reward.

2

But when thou doest alms, let not thy left hand know what thy right hand doeth: 3

That thine alms may be in secret: and thy Father which seeth in secret himself shall reward thee openly. 4

Moreover when ye fast, be not, as the hypocrites, of a sad countenance: for they disfigure their faces, that they may appear unto men to fast. Verily I say unto you, They have their reward. 16

But thou, when thou fastest, anoint thine head, and wash thy face; 17

That thou appear not unto men to fast, but unto thy Father which is in secret: and thy Father, which seeth in secret, shall reward thee openly. 18

And when thou prayest, thou shalt not be as the hypocrites are: for they love to pray standing in the synagogues and in the corners of the streets, that they may be seen of men. Verily I say unto you, They have their reward. 5

But thou, when thou prayest, enter into thy closet, and when thou hast shut thy door, pray to thy Father which is in secret; and thy Father which seeth in secret shall reward thee openly. 6

But when ye pray, use not vain repetitions, as the heathen do: for they think that they shall be heard for their much speaking. 7

Be not ye therefore like unto them: for your Father knoweth what things ye have need of, before ye ask him. 8

After this manner therefore pray ye: Our Father which art in heaven, Hallowed be thy name. 9

Thy kingdom come. Thy will be done in earth, as it is in heaven. 10

Give us this day our daily bread.                                    11

And forgive us our debts, as we forgive our debt-        12
ors.

And lead us not into temptation, but deliver us          13
from evil: For thine is the kingdom, and the power,
and the glory, for ever. Amen.

For if ye forgive men their trespasses, your heav-       14
enly Father will also forgive you:

But if ye forgive not men their trespasses, neither      15
will your Father forgive your trespasses.


## Redemption and the Forgiveness of Sins

Verily, verily, I say unto thee, Except a man be born     Jn 3: 3
again, he cannot see the kingdom of God.


[Only] ask, and it shall be given you; seek, and         Mt 7: 7
ye shall find; knock, and it shall be opened unto
you:

For every one that asketh receiveth; and he that              8
seeketh findeth; and to him that knocketh it shall
be opened.


For the kingdom of heaven is like unto a man that        Mt 20: 1
is an householder, which went out early in the
morning to hire labourers into his vineyard.

And when he had agreed with the labourers for a               2
penny a day, he sent them into his vineyard.

And he went out about the third hour, and saw                3
others standing idle in the marketplace,

And said unto them; Go ye also into the vineyard,             4
and whatsoever is right I will give you. And they
went their way.

Again he went out about the sixth and ninth hour, and did likewise. 5

And about the eleventh hour he went out, and found others standing idle, and saith unto them, Why stand ye here all the day idle? 6

They say unto him, Because no man hath hired us. He saith unto them, Go ye also into the vineyard; and whatsoever is right, that shall ye receive. 7

So when even was come, the lord of the vineyard saith unto his steward, Call the labourers, and give them their hire, beginning from the last unto the first. 8

And when they came that were hired about the eleventh hour, they received every man a penny. 9

But when the first came, they supposed that they should have received more; and they likewise received every man a penny. 10

And when they had received it, they murmured against the goodman of the house, 11

Saying, These last have wrought but one hour, and thou hast made them equal unto us, which have borne the burden and heat of the day. 12

But he answered one of them, and said, Friend, I do thee no wrong: didst not thou agree with me for a penny? 13

Take that thine is, and go thy way: I will give unto this last, even as unto thee. 14

Is it not lawful for me to do what I will with mine own? Is thine eye evil, because I am good? 15

So the last shall be first, and the first last: for many be called, but few chosen. 16

Or what man is there of you, whom if his son ask bread, will he give him a stone?

Mt 7: 9

Or if he ask a fish, will he give him a serpent?

10

If ye then, being evil, know how to give good gifts unto your children, how much more shall your Father which is in heaven give good things to them that ask him?

11

## Temptation and False Prophets

Enter ye in at the strait gate: for wide is the gate, and broad is the way, that leadeth to destruction, and many there be which go in thereat:

Mt 7:13

Because strait is the gate, and narrow is the way, which leadeth unto life, and few there be that find it.

14

Beware of false prophets, which come to you in sheep's clothing, but inwardly they are ravening wolves.

15

Ye shall know them by their fruits. Do men gather grapes of thorns, or figs of thistles?

16

Even so every good tree bringeth forth good fruit; but a corrupt tree bringeth forth evil fruit.

17

Every tree that bringeth not forth good fruit is hewn down, and cast into the fire.

19

Wherefore by their fruits ye shall know them.

20

Not every one that saith unto me, Lord, Lord, shall enter into the kingdom of heaven; but he that doeth the will of my Father which is in heaven.

21

Many will say to me in that day, Lord, Lord, have we not prophesied in thy name? and in thy name

22

have cast out devils? and in thy name done many wonderful works?

And then will I profess unto them, I never knew you: depart from me, ye that work iniquity.   23

Therefore whosoever heareth these sayings of mine, and doeth them, I will liken him unto a wise man, which built his house upon a rock:   24

And the rain descended, and the floods came, and the winds blew, and beat upon that house; and it fell not: for it was founded upon a rock.   25

And every one that heareth these sayings of mine, and doeth them not, shall be likened unto a foolish man, which built his house upon the sand:   26

And the rain descended, and the floods came, and the winds blew, and beat upon that house; and it fell: and great was the fall of it.   27

## Crucifixion and Resurrection

Let these sayings sink down into your ears: for the Son of man shall be delivered into the hands of men.   Lk 9:44

And they shall kill him, and the third day he shall be raised again.   Mt 17:23

Behold, we go up to Jerusalem, and all things that are written by the prophets concerning the Son of man shall be accomplished.   Lk 18:31

For he shall be delivered unto the Gentiles, and shall be mocked, and spitefully entreated, and spitted on:   32

And they shall scourge him, and put him to death: and the third day he shall rise again.

33

The Son of man goeth as it is written of him: but woe unto that man by whom the Son of man is betrayed! it had been good for that man if he had not been born.

Mt 26:24

Sit ye here, while I go and pray yonder.

Mt 26:36

My soul is exceeding sorrowful, even unto death: tarry ye here, and watch with me [while I pray].

Mt 26:38

O my Father, if it be possible, let this cup pass from me: nevertheless not as I will, but as thou wilt.

Mt 26:39

O my Father, if this cup may not pass away from me, except I drink it, thy will be done.

42

*[Turning to a disciple]* Put up again thy sword into his place: for all they that take the sword shall perish with the sword.

52

Thinkest thou that I cannot now pray to my Father, and he shall presently give me more than twelve legions of angels?

53

But how then shall the scriptures be fulfilled, that thus it must be?

54

My kingdom is not of this world: if my kingdom were of this world, then would my servants fight, that I should not be delivered [to my enemies]: but now is my kingdom not from hence.

Jn 18:36

Thou sayest that I am a king. To this end was I born, and for this cause came I into the world, that

37

I should bear witness unto the truth. Every one that
is of the truth heareth my voice.

Daughters of Jerusalem, weep not for me, but weep     Lk 23:28
for yourselves, and for your children.

For, behold, the days are coming, in the which     29
they shall say, Blessed are the barren, and the
wombs that never bare, and the paps which never
gave suck.

Then shall they begin to say to the mountains, Fall     30
on us; and to the hills, Cover us.

For if they do these things in a green tree, what     31
shall be done in the dry?

Father, forgive them; for they know not what they     Lk 23:34
do.

Eli, Eli, lama sabachthani? *that is to say, My God,*     Mt 27:46
*my God, why hast thou forsaken me?*

Father, into thy hands I commend my spirit.     Lk 23:46

It is finished.     Jn 19:30

Thus it is written, and thus it behoved Christ to     Lk 24:46
suffer, and to rise from the dead the third day:

And that repentance and remission of sins should     47
be preached in his name among all nations, beginning at Jerusalem.

And ye are witnesses of these things.     48

And, behold, I send you the promise of my Father     49
upon you: but tarry ye in the city of Jerusalem, until
ye be endued with power from on high.

I am the resurrection, and the life: he that believeth in me, though he were dead, yet shall he live:

Jn 11:25

And whosoever liveth and believeth in me shall never die....

26

For God so loved the world, that he gave his only begotten Son, that whosoever believeth in him should not perish, but have everlasting life.

Jn 3:16

...God sent not his Son into the world to condemn the world; but that the world through him might be saved.

17

These things I have spoken unto you, that in me ye might have peace. In the world ye shall have tribulation: but be of good cheer; I have overcome the world.

Jn 16:33

## The Gift of the Holy Spirit

Whither I go, thou canst not follow me now; but thou shalt follow me afterwards.

Jn 13:36

It is not for you to know the times or the seasons, which the Father hath put in his own power.

Ac 1: 7

But ye shall receive power, after that the Holy Ghost is come upon you: and ye shall be witnesses unto me both in Jerusalem, and in all Judaea, and in Samaria, and unto the uttermost part of the earth.

8

[For] Satan hath desired to have you, that he may sift you as wheat:

Lk 22:31

But I have prayed for [you], that [your] faith fail          32
not: and when [you are] converted, strengthen
[your] brethren.

The harvest truly is plenteous, but the labourers      Mt 9:37
are few....

Go ye therefore, and teach all nations, baptizing     Mt 28:19
them in the name of the Father, and of the Son,
and of the Holy Ghost:

Teaching them to observe all things whatsoever I       20
have commanded you....

But beware of men: for they will deliver you up to    Mt 10:17
the councils, and they will scourge you in their synagogues;

Behold, I send you forth as sheep in the midst of      16
wolves: be ye therefore wise as serpents, and harmless as doves.

But when they deliver you up, take no thought how      19
or what ye shall speak: for it shall be given you in
that same hour what ye shall speak.

For it is not ye that speak, but the Spirit of your    20
Father which speaketh in you.

And fear not them which kill the body, but are not     28
able to kill the soul: but rather fear him which is
able to destroy both soul and body in hell.

[For] verily I say unto you, There is no man that     Lk 18:29
hath left house, or parents, or brethren, or wife, or
children, for the kingdom of God's sake,

Who shall not receive manifold more in this present    30
time, and in the world to come life everlasting.

# The Second Coming

Take heed that no man deceive you.                    Mt 24: 4

For many shall come in my name, saying, I am          5
Christ; and shall deceive many.

And ye shall hear of wars and rumours of wars: see    6
that ye be not troubled: for all these things must
come to pass, but the end is not yet.

For nation shall rise against nation, and king-       7
dom against kingdom: and there shall be famines, and pestilences, and earthquakes, in divers
places.

And then shall many be offended, and shall betray     10
one another, and shall hate one another.

And because iniquity shall abound, the love of many   12
shall wax cold.

But he that shall endure unto the end, the same       13
shall be saved.

For as the lightning cometh out of the east, and      27
shineth even unto the west; so shall also the coming of the Son of man be.

Immediately after the tribulation of those days       29
shall the sun be darkened, and the moon shall
not give her light, and the stars shall fall from
heaven, and the powers of the heavens shall be
shaken:

And then shall appear the sign of the Son of man      30
in heaven: and then shall all the tribes of the earth
mourn, and they shall see the Son of man coming in the clouds of heaven with power and great
glory.

And he shall send his angels with a great sound of a  31
trumpet, and they shall gather together his elect

from the four winds, from one end of heaven to the other.

Then shall the King say unto them on his right hand, Come, ye blessed of my Father, inherit the kingdom prepared for you from the foundation of the world:

Mt 25:34

For I was an hungred, and ye gave me meat: I was thirsty, and ye gave me drink: I was a stranger, and ye took me in:

35

Naked, and ye clothed me: I was sick, and ye visited me: I was in prison, and ye came unto me.

36

Then shall the righteous answer him, saying, Lord, when saw we thee an hungred, and fed thee? or thirsty, and gave thee drink?

37

When saw we thee a stranger, and took thee in? or naked, and clothed thee?

38

Or when saw we thee sick, or in prison, and came unto thee?

39

And the King shall answer and say unto them, Verily I say unto you, Inasmuch as ye have done it unto one of the least of these my brethren, ye have done it unto me.

40

Then shall he say also unto them on the left hand, Depart from me, ye cursed, into everlasting fire, prepared for the devil and his angels:

41

For I was an hungred, and ye gave me no meat: I was thirsty, and ye gave me no drink:

42

I was a stranger, and ye took me not in: naked, and ye clothed me not: sick, and in prison, and ye visited me not.

43

Then shall they also answer him, saying, Lord, when 44
saw we thee an hungred, or athirst, or a stranger, or
naked, or sick, or in prison, and did not minister
unto thee?

Then shall he answer them, saying, Verily I say unto 45
you, Inasmuch as ye did it not to one of the least of
these, ye did it not to me.

## Conclusion

Father, the hour is come.... Jn 17: 1

While I was with them in the world, I kept them in 12
thy name: those that thou gavest me I have kept,
and none of them is lost, but the son of perdition;
that the scripture might be fulfilled.

And now come I to thee; and these things I speak 13
in the world, that they might have my joy fulfilled
in themselves.

I have given them thy word; and the world hath 14
hated them, because they are not of the world, even
as I am not of the world.

I pray not that thou shouldest take them out of the 15
world, but that thou shouldest keep them from the
evil.

Sanctify them through thy truth: thy word is truth. 17

As thou hast sent me into the world, even so have I 18
also sent them into the world.

And for their sakes I sanctify myself, that they also 19
might be sanctified through the truth.

Neither pray I for these alone, but for them also 20
which shall believe on me through their word;

That they all may be one; as thou, Father, art in me, and I in thee, that they also may be one in us: that the world may believe that thou hast sent me.

21

And I have declared unto them thy name, and will declare it: that the love wherewith thou hast loved me may be in them, and I in them.

26

These things have I spoken unto you, that my joy might remain in you, and that your joy might be full.

Jn 15: 11

Blessed are the poor in spirit: for theirs is the kingdom of heaven.

Mt 5: 3

Blessed are they that mourn: for they shall be comforted.

4

Blessed are the meek: for they shall inherit the earth.

5

Blessed are they which do hunger and thirst after righteousness: for they shall be filled.

6

Blessed are the merciful: for they shall obtain mercy.

7

Blessed are the pure in heart: for they shall see God.

8

Blessed are the peacemakers: for they shall be called the children of God.

9

Blessed are they which are persecuted for righteousness' sake: for theirs is the kingdom of heaven.

10

Ye are the salt of the earth: but if the salt have lost his savour, wherewith shall it be salted? it is thenceforth good for nothing, but to be cast out, and to be trodden under foot of men.

Mt 5: 13

Ye are the light of the world. A city that is set on an hill cannot be hid. 14

Neither do men light a candle, and put it under a bushel, but on a candlestick; and it giveth light unto all that are in the house. 15

Let your light so shine before men, that they may see your good works, and glorify your Father which is in heaven. 16

# PART II

# Other Important Sayings

## The Gospel According to St. Matthew

Give not that which is holy unto the dogs, neither cast ye your pearls before swine, lest they trample them under their feet, and turn again and rend you.  7: 6

The foxes have holes, and the birds of the air have nests; but the Son of man hath not where to lay his head.  8:20

[G]o ye and learn what that meaneth, I will have mercy, and not sacrifice: for I am not come to call the righteous, but sinners to repentance.  9:13

No man putteth a piece of new cloth unto an old garment, for that which is put in to fill it up taketh from the garment, and the rent is made worse.  9:16

Neither do men put new wine into old bottles: else the bottles break, and the wine runneth out, and the bottles perish: but they put new wine into new bottles, and both are preserved.  17

Daughter, be of good comfort; thy faith hath made thee whole.  9:22

Go not into the way of the Gentiles, and into any city of the Samaritans enter ye not:  10: 5

But go rather to the lost sheep of the house of Israel.  6

And as ye go, preach, saying, The kingdom of heaven is at hand.  7

Heal the sick, cleanse the lepers, raise the dead, cast out devils: freely ye have received, freely give.  8

Provide neither gold, nor silver, nor brass in your purses,  9

Nor scrip for your journey, neither two coats, neither shoes, nor yet staves: for the workman is worthy of his meat.  10

And into whatsoever city or town ye shall enter, enquire who in it is worthy; and there abide till ye go thence.  11

And when ye come into an house, salute it.  12

And if the house be worthy, let your peace come upon it: but if it be not worthy, let your peace return to you.  13

And whosoever shall not receive you, nor hear your words, when ye depart out of that house or city, shake off the dust of your feet.  14

Verily I say unto you, It shall be more tolerable for the land of Sodom and Gomorrha in the day of judgment, than for that city.  15

And ye shall be brought before governors and kings for my sake, for a testimony against them and the Gentiles.  18

And the brother shall deliver up the brother to death, and the father the child: and the children shall rise up against their parents, and cause them to be put to death.  21

And ye shall be hated of all men for my name's sake: but he that endureth to the end shall be saved.  22

But when they persecute you in this city, flee ye into another: for verily I say unto you, Ye shall not have gone over the cities of Israel, till the Son of man be come. 23

The disciple is not above his master, nor the servant above his lord. 24

It is enough for the disciple that he be as his master, and the servant as his lord. If they have called the master of the house Beelzebub, how much more shall they call them of his household? 25

Whosoever therefore shall confess me before men, him will I confess also before my Father which is in heaven. 32

But whosoever shall deny me before men, him will I also deny before my Father which is in heaven. 33

Think not that I am come to send peace on earth: I came not to send peace, but a sword. 34

For I am come to set a man at variance against his father, and the daughter against her mother, and the daughter in law against her mother in law. 35

And a man's foes shall be they of his own household. 36

He that loveth father or mother more than me is not worthy of me: and he that loveth son or daughter more than me is not worthy of me. 37

And he that taketh not his cross, and followeth after me, is not worthy of me. 38

He that findeth his life shall lose it: and he that loseth his life for my sake shall find it. 39

He that receiveth you receiveth me, and he that receiveth me receiveth him that sent me. 40

He that receiveth a prophet in the name of a prophet shall receive a prophet's reward; and he that receiveth 41 a righteous man in the name of a righteous man shall receive a righteous man's reward.

And whosoever shall give to drink unto one of these little ones a cup of cold water only in the name of a disciple, verily I say unto you, he shall in no wise lose his reward. 42

What man shall there be among you, that shall have one sheep, and if it fall into a pit on the sabbath day, will he not lay hold on it, and lift it out? 12:11

How much then is a man better than a sheep? Wherefore it is lawful to do well on the sabbath days. 12

Every kingdom divided against itself is brought to desolation; and every city or house divided against itself shall not stand: 12:25

And if Satan cast out Satan, he is divided against himself; how shall then his kingdom stand? 26

And if I by Beelzebub cast out devils, by whom do your children cast them out? therefore they shall be your judges. 27

But if I cast out devils by the Spirit of God, then the kingdom of God is come unto you. 28

Or else how can one enter into a strong man's house, and spoil his goods, except he first bind the strong man? and then he will spoil his house. 29

He that is not with me is against me; and he that gathereth not with me scattereth abroad. 30

Wherefore I say unto you, All manner of sin and blasphemy shall be forgiven unto men: but the blasphemy against the Holy Ghost shall not be forgiven unto men. 31

O generation of vipers, how can ye, being evil, speak good things? for out of the abundance of the heart the mouth speaketh.

12:34

For by thy words thou shalt be justified, and by thy words thou shalt be condemned.

37

Behold, a sower went forth to sow;

13: 3

And when he sowed, some seeds fell by the way side, and the fowls came and devoured them up:

4

Some fell upon stony places, where they had not much earth: and forthwith they sprung up, because they had no deepness of earth:

5

And when the sun was up, they were scorched; and because they had no root, they withered away.

6

And some fell among thorns; and the thorns sprung up, and choked them:

7

But other fell into good ground, and brought forth fruit, some an hundredfold, some sixtyfold, some thirtyfold.

8

Who hath ears to hear, let him hear.

9

Because it is given unto you to know the mysteries of the kingdom of heaven, but to them it is not given.

11

For whosoever hath, to him shall be given, and he shall have more abundance: but whosoever hath not, from him shall be taken away even that he hath.

12

Therefore speak I to them in parables: because they seeing see not; and hearing they hear not, neither do they understand.

13

And in them is fulfilled the prophecy of Esaias, which saith, By hearing ye shall hear, and shall not understand; and seeing ye shall see, and shall not perceive:

14

For this people's heart is waxed gross, and their ears 15
are dull of hearing, and their eyes they have closed;
lest at any time they should see with their eyes, and
hear with their ears, and should understand with
their heart, and should be converted, and I should
heal them.

But blessed are your eyes, for they see: and your 16
ears, for they hear.

For verily I say unto you, That many prophets and 17
righteous men have desired to see those things
which ye see, and have not seen them; and to hear
those things which ye hear, and have not heard
them.

Hear ye therefore the parable of the sower. 18

When any one heareth the word of the kingdom, 19
and understandeth it not, then cometh the wicked
one, and catcheth away that which was sown in his
heart. This is he which received seed by the way
side.

But he that received the seed into stony places, the 20
same is he that heareth the word, and anon with
joy receiveth it;

Yet hath he not root in himself, but dureth for a 21
while: for when tribulation or persecution ariseth
because of the word, by and by he is offended.

He also that received seed among the thorns is he 22
that heareth the word; and the care of this world,
and the deceitfulness of riches, choke the word, and
he becometh unfruitful.

But he that received seed into the good ground is 23
he that heareth the word, and understandeth it;
which also beareth fruit, and bringeth forth, some
an hundredfold, some sixty, some thirty.

The kingdom of heaven is likened unto a man which 24
sowed good seed in his field:

But while men slept, his enemy came and sowed tares among the wheat, and went his way. 25

But when the blade was sprung up, and brought forth fruit, then appeared the tares also. 26

So the servants of the householder came and said unto him, Sir, didst not thou sow good seed in thy field? from whence then hath it tares? 27

He said unto them, An enemy hath done this. The servants said unto him, Wilt thou then that we go and gather them up? 28

But he said, Nay; lest while ye gather up the tares, ye root up also the wheat with them. 29

Let both grow together until the harvest: and in the time of harvest I will say to the reapers, Gather ye together first the tares, and bind them in bundles to burn them: but gather the wheat into my barn. 30

The kingdom of heaven is like to a grain of mustard seed, which a man took, and sowed in his field: 31

Which indeed is the least of all seeds: but when it is grown, it is the greatest among herbs, and becometh a tree, so that the birds of the air come and lodge in the branches thereof. 32

The kingdom of heaven is like unto leaven, which a woman took, and hid in three measures of meal, till the whole was leavened. 33

He that soweth the good seed is the Son of man; 37

The field is the world; the good seed are the children of the kingdom; but the tares are the children of the wicked one; 38

The enemy that sowed them is the devil; the harvest is the end of the world; and the reapers are the angels. 39

As therefore the tares are gathered and burned in the fire; so shall it be in the end of this world.    40

The Son of man shall send forth his angels, and they shall gather out of his kingdom all things that offend, and them which do iniquity;    41

And shall cast them into a furnace of fire: there shall be wailing and gnashing of teeth.    42

Then shall the righteous shine forth as the sun in the kingdom of their Father. Who hath ears to hear, let him hear.    43

Again, the kingdom of heaven is like unto treasure hid in a field; the which when a man hath found, he hideth, and for joy thereof goeth and selleth all that he hath, and buyeth that field.    44

Again, the kingdom of heaven is like unto a merchant man, seeking goodly pearls:    45

Who, when he had found one pearl of great price, went and sold all that he had, and bought it.    46

Again, the kingdom of heaven is like unto a net, that was cast into the sea, and gathered of every kind:    47

Which, when it was full, they drew to shore, and sat down, and gathered the good into vessels, but cast the bad away.    48

So shall it be at the end of the world: the angels shall come forth, and sever the wicked from among the just,    49

And shall cast them into the furnace of fire: there shall be wailing and gnashing of teeth.    50

Have ye understood all these things?    51

A prophet is not without honour, save in his own country, and in his own house.    13:57

O thou of little faith, wherefore didst thou doubt?            14:31

Not that which goeth into the mouth defileth a man;            15:11
but that which cometh out of the mouth, this
defileth a man.

Every plant, which my heavenly Father hath not                13
planted, shall be rooted up.

Let them alone: they be blind leaders of the blind.           14
And if the blind lead the blind, both shall fall into
the ditch.

Do not ye yet understand, that whatsoever entereth            17
in at the mouth goeth into the belly, and is cast out
into the draught?

But those things which proceed out of the mouth               18
come forth from the heart; and they defile the man.

For out of the heart proceed evil thoughts, mur-              19
ders, adulteries, fornications, thefts, false witness,
blasphemies:

These are the things which defile a man: but to eat           20
with unwashen hands defileth not a man.

It is not meet to take the children's bread, and to           15:26
cast it to dogs.

And I say also unto thee, That thou art Peter, and            16:18
upon this rock I will build my church; and the gates
of hell shall not prevail against it.

Get thee behind me, Satan: thou art an offence unto           23
me: for thou savourest not the things that be of God,
but those that be of men.

For the Son of man shall come in the glory of his             27
Father with his angels; and then he shall reward every man according to his works.

Verily I say unto you, There be some standing here, which shall not taste of death, till they see the Son of man coming in his kingdom.  28

[F]or verily I say unto you, If ye have faith as a grain of mustard seed, ye shall say unto this mountain, Remove hence to yonder place; and it shall remove; and nothing shall be impossible unto you.  17:20

The Son of man shall be betrayed into the hands of men.  17:22

Verily I say unto you, Except ye be converted, and become as little children, ye shall not enter into the kingdom of heaven.  18: 3

Whosoever therefore shall humble himself as this little child, the same is greatest in the kingdom of heaven.  4

And whoso shall receive one such little child in my name receiveth me.  5

But whoso shall offend one of these little ones which believe in me, it were better for him that a millstone were hanged about his neck, and that he were drowned in the depth of the sea.  6

Wherefore if thy hand or thy foot offend thee, cut them off, and cast them from thee: it is better for thee to enter into life halt or maimed, rather than having two hands or two feet to be cast into everlasting fire.  8

And if thine eye offend thee, pluck it out, and cast it from thee: it is better for thee to enter into life with one eye, rather than having two eyes to be cast into hell fire.  9

For the Son of man is come to save that which was lost.  18:11

How think ye? if a man have an hundred sheep, and one of them be gone astray, doth he not leave the ninety and nine, and goeth into the mountains, and seeketh that which is gone astray? 12

And if so be that he find it, verily I say unto you, he rejoiceth more of that sheep, than of the ninety and nine which went not astray. 13

Even so it is not the will of your Father which is in heaven, that one of these little ones should perish. 14

Moreover if thy brother shall trespass against thee, go and tell him his fault between thee and him alone: if he shall hear thee, thou hast gained thy brother. 15

But if he will not hear thee, then take with thee one or two more, that in the mouth of two or three witnesses every word may be established. 16

And if he shall neglect to hear them, tell it unto the church: but if he neglect to hear the church, let him be unto thee as an heathen man and a publican. 17

For where two or three are gathered together in my name, there am I in the midst of them. 18:20

Therefore is the kingdom of heaven likened unto a certain king, which would take account of his servants. 18:23

And when he had begun to reckon, one was brought unto him, which owed him ten thousand talents. 24

But forasmuch as he had not to pay, his lord commanded him to be sold, and his wife, and children, and all that he had, and payment to be made. 25

The servant therefore fell down, and worshipped him, saying, Lord, have patience with me, and I will pay thee all. 26

Then the lord of that servant was moved with compassion, and loosed him, and forgave him the debt.

27

But the same servant went out, and found one of
his fellowservants, which owed him an hundred
pence: and he laid hands on him, and took him by
the throat, saying, Pay me that thou owest.

28

And his fellowservant fell down at his feet, and besought him, saying, Have patience with me, and I
will pay thee all.

29

And he would not: but went and cast him into
prison, till he should pay the debt.

30

So when his fellowservants saw what was done, they
were very sorry, and came and told unto their lord
all that was done.

31

Then his lord, after that he had called him, said
unto him, O thou wicked servant, I forgave thee all
that debt, because thou desiredst me:

32

Shouldest not thou also have had compassion on
thy fellowservant, even as I had pity on thee?

33

And his lord was wroth, and delivered him to the
tormentors, till he should pay all that was due unto
him.

34

So likewise shall my heavenly Father do also unto
you, if ye from your hearts forgive not every one his
brother their trespasses.

35

Have ye not read, that he which made them at the
beginning made them male and female,

19: 4

And said, For this cause shall a man leave father
and mother, and shall cleave to his wife: and they
twain shall be one flesh?

5

Wherefore they are no more twain, but one flesh.
What therefore God hath joined together, let not
man put asunder.

6

Moses because of the hardness of your hearts suffered you to put away your wives: but from the beginning it was not so.   8

And I say unto you, Whosoever shall put away his wife, except it be for fornication, and shall marry another, committeth adultery: and whoso marrieth her which is put away doth commit adultery.   9

Why callest thou me good? there is none good but one, that is, God: but if thou wilt enter into life, keep the commandments.   19:17

Thou shalt do no murder, Thou shalt not commit adultery, Thou shalt not steal, Thou shalt not bear false witness,   18

Honour thy father and thy mother: and, Thou shalt love thy neighbour as thyself.   19

And all things, whatsoever ye shall ask in prayer, believing, ye shall receive.   21:22

But what think ye? A certain man had two sons; and he came to the first, and said, Son, go work to day in my vineyard.   21:28

He answered and said, I will not: but afterward he repented, and went.   29

And he came to the second, and said likewise. And he answered and said, I go, sir: and went not.   30

Whether of them twain did the will of his father? Verily I say unto you, That the publicans and the harlots go into the kingdom of God before you.   31

Hear another parable: There was a certain householder, which planted a vineyard, and hedged it   21:33

round about, and digged a winepress in it, and built a tower, and let it out to husbandmen, and went into a far country:

And when the time of the fruit drew near, he sent his servants to the husbandmen, that they might receive the fruits of it. 34

And the husbandmen took his servants, and beat one, and killed another, and stoned another. 35

Again, he sent other servants more than the first: and they did unto them likewise. 36

But last of all he sent unto them his son, saying, They will reverence my son. 37

But when the husbandmen saw the son, they said among themselves, This is the heir; come, let us kill him, and let us seize on his inheritance. 38

And they caught him, and cast him out of the vineyard, and slew him. 39

When the lord therefore of the vineyard cometh, what will he do unto those husbandmen? 40

Did ye never read in the scriptures, The stone which the builders rejected, the same is become the head of the corner: this is the Lord's doing, and it is marvellous in our eyes? 42

Therefore say I unto you, The kingdom of God shall be taken from you, and given to a nation bringing forth the fruits thereof. 43

The kingdom of heaven is like unto a certain king, which made a marriage for his son, 22: 2

And sent forth his servants to call them that were bidden to the wedding: and they would not come. 3

Again, he sent forth other servants, saying, Tell them which are bidden, Behold, I have prepared my din- 4 ner: my oxen and my fatlings are killed, and all things are ready: come unto the marriage.

But they made light of it, and went their ways, one to his farm, another to his merchandise: 5

And the remnant took his servants, and entreated them spitefully, and slew them. 6

But when the king heard thereof, he was wroth: and he sent forth his armies, and destroyed those murderers, and burned up their city. 7

Then saith he to his servants, The wedding is ready, but they which were bidden were not worthy. 8

Go ye therefore into the highways, and as many as ye shall find, bid to the marriage. 9

So those servants went out into the highways, and gathered together all as many as they found, both bad and good: and the wedding was furnished with guests. 10

And when the king came in to see the guests, he saw there a man which had not on a wedding garment: 11

And he saith unto him, Friend, how camest thou in hither not having a wedding garment? And he was speechless. 12

Then said the king to the servants, Bind him hand and foot, and take him away, and cast him into outer darkness; there shall be weeping and gnashing of teeth. 13

For many are called, but few are chosen. 14

Shew me the tribute money. 22:19

Whose is this image and superscription? 20

Render therefore unto Caesar the things which are Caesar's; and unto God the things that are God's. 21

For in the resurrection they neither marry, nor are given in marriage, but are as the angels of God in heaven.

22:30

The scribes and the Pharisees sit in Moses' seat:

23: 2

All therefore whatsoever they bid you observe, that observe and do; but do not ye after their works: for they say, and do not.

3

For they bind heavy burdens and grievous to be borne, and lay them on men's shoulders; but they themselves will not move them with one of their fingers.

4

But all their works they do for to be seen of men: they make broad their phylacteries, and enlarge the borders of their garments,

5

And love the uppermost rooms at feasts, and the chief seats in the synagogues,

6

And greetings in the markets, and to be called of men, Rabbi, Rabbi.

7

But be not ye called Rabbi: for one is your Master, even Christ; and all ye are brethren.

8

And call no man your father upon the earth: for one is your Father, which is in heaven.

9

Neither be ye called masters: for one is your Master, even Christ.

10

But he that is greatest among you shall be your servant.

11

And whosoever shall exalt himself shall be abased; and he that shall humble himself shall be exalted.

12

But woe unto you, scribes and Pharisees, hypocrites! for ye shut up the kingdom of heaven against men: for ye neither go in yourselves, neither suffer ye them that are entering to go in.

13

Woe unto you, scribes and Pharisees, hypocrites! for ye devour widows' houses, and for a pretence make long prayer: therefore ye shall receive the greater damnation. 14

Woe unto you, scribes and Pharisees, hypocrites! for ye compass sea and land to make one proselyte, and when he is made, ye make him twofold more the child of hell than yourselves. 15

Woe unto you, ye blind guides, which say, Whosoever shall swear by the temple, it is nothing; but whosoever shall swear by the gold of the temple, he is a debtor! 16

Ye fools and blind: for whether is greater, the gold, or the temple that sanctifieth the gold? 17

And, Whosoever shall swear by the altar, it is nothing; but whosoever sweareth by the gift that is upon it, he is guilty. 18

Ye fools and blind: for whether is greater, the gift, or the altar that sanctifieth the gift? 19

Whoso therefore shall swear by the altar, sweareth by it, and by all things thereon. 20

And whoso shall swear by the temple, sweareth by it, and by him that dwelleth therein. 21

And he that shall swear by heaven, sweareth by the throne of God, and by him that sitteth thereon. 22

Woe unto you, scribes and Pharisees, hypocrites! for ye pay tithe of mint and anise and cummin, and have omitted the weightier matters of the law, judgment, mercy, and faith: these ought ye to have done, and not to leave the other undone. 23

Ye blind guides, which strain at a gnat, and swallow a camel. 24

Woe unto you, scribes and Pharisees, hypocrites! for ye make clean the outside of the cup and of the 25 platter, but within they are full of extortion and excess.

Thou blind Pharisee, cleanse first that which is within the cup and platter, that the outside of them may be clean also.    26

Woe unto you, scribes and Pharisees, hypocrites! for ye are like unto whited sepulchres, which indeed appear beautiful outward, but are within full of dead men's bones, and of all uncleanness.    27

Even so ye also outwardly appear righteous unto men, but within ye are full of hypocrisy and iniquity.    28

Woe unto you, scribes and Pharisees, hypocrites! because ye build the tombs of the prophets, and garnish the sepulchres of the righteous.    29

Ye serpents, ye generation of vipers, how can ye escape the damnation of hell?    33

Wherefore, behold, I send unto you prophets, and wise men, and scribes: and some of them ye shall kill and crucify; and some of them shall ye scourge in your synagogues, and persecute them from city to city:    34

That upon you may come all the righteous blood shed upon the earth, from the blood of righteous Abel unto the blood of Zacharias son of Barachias, whom ye slew between the temple and the altar.    35

Verily I say unto you, All these things shall come upon this generation.    36

O Jerusalem, Jerusalem, thou that killest the prophets, and stonest them which are sent unto thee, how often would I have gathered thy children together, even as a hen gathereth her chickens under her wings, and ye would not!    37

Behold, your house is left unto you desolate.    38

For I say unto you, Ye shall not see me henceforth, till ye shall say, Blessed is he that cometh in the name of the Lord.  39

See ye not all these things? verily I say unto you, There shall not be left here one stone upon another, that shall not be thrown down.  24: 2

All these are the beginning of sorrows.  24: 8

Then shall they deliver you up to be afflicted, and shall kill you: and ye shall be hated of all nations for my name's sake.  9

And many false prophets shall rise, and shall deceive many.  11

And this gospel of the kingdom shall be preached in all the world for a witness unto all nations; and then shall the end come.  14

When ye therefore shall see the abomination of desolation, spoken of by Daniel the prophet, stand in the holy place,  15

Then let them which be in Judaea flee into the mountains:  16

Let him which is on the housetop not come down to take any thing out of his house:  17

Neither let him which is in the field return back to take his clothes.  18

And woe unto them that are with child, and to them that give suck in those days!  19

But pray ye that your flight be not in the winter, neither on the sabbath day:  20

For then shall be great tribulation, such as was not since the beginning of the world to this time, no, nor ever shall be.  21

And except those days should be shortened, there should no flesh be saved: but for the elect's sake those days shall be shortened.  22

Then if any man shall say unto you, Lo, here is Christ, or there; believe it not.  23

For there shall arise false Christs, and false prophets, and shall shew great signs and wonders; insomuch that, if it were possible, they shall deceive the very elect.  24

Behold, I have told you before.  25

Wherefore if they shall say unto you, Behold, he is in the desert; go not forth: behold, he is in the secret chambers; believe it not.  26

Now learn a parable of the fig tree; When his branch is yet tender, and putteth forth leaves, ye know that summer is nigh:  24:32

So likewise ye, when ye shall see all these things, know that it is near, even at the doors.  33

Verily I say unto you, This generation shall not pass, till all these things be fulfilled.  34

Heaven and earth shall pass away, but my words shall not pass away.  35

But of that day and hour knoweth no man, no, not the angels of heaven, but my Father only.  36

But as the days of Noe were, so shall also the coming of the Son of man be.  37

For as in the days that were before the flood they were eating and drinking, marrying and giving in marriage, until the day that Noe entered into the ark,  38

And knew not until the flood came, and took them all away; so shall also the coming of the Son of man be.  39

Then shall two be in the field; the one shall be taken, and the other left. 40

Two women shall be grinding at the mill; the one shall be taken, and the other left. 41

Watch therefore: for ye know not what hour your Lord doth come. 42

But know this, that if the goodman of the house had known in what watch the thief would come, he would have watched, and would not have suffered his house to be broken up. 43

Therefore be ye also ready: for in such an hour as ye think not the Son of man cometh. 44

Who then is a faithful and wise servant, whom his lord hath made ruler over his household, to give them meat in due season? 45

Blessed is that servant, whom his lord when he cometh shall find so doing. 46

Verily I say unto you, That he shall make him ruler over all his goods. 47

But and if that evil servant shall say in his heart, My lord delayeth his coming; 48

And shall begin to smite his fellowservants, and to eat and drink with the drunken; 49

The lord of that servant shall come in a day when he looketh not for him, and in an hour that he is not aware of, 50

And shall cut him asunder, and appoint him his portion with the hypocrites: there shall be weeping and gnashing of teeth. 51

Then shall the kingdom of heaven be likened unto ten virgins, which took their lamps, and went forth to meet the bridegroom. 25: 1

And five of them were wise, and five were foolish.　2

They that were foolish took their lamps, and took　3
no oil with them:

But the wise took oil in their vessels with their lamps.　4

While the bridegroom tarried, they all slumbered　5
and slept.

And at midnight there was a cry made, Behold, the　6
bridegroom cometh; go ye out to meet him.

Then all those virgins arose, and trimmed their　7
lamps.

And the foolish said unto the wise, Give us of your　8
oil; for our lamps are gone out.

But the wise answered, saying, Not so; lest there be　9
not enough for us and you: but go ye rather to them
that sell, and buy for yourselves.

And while they went to buy, the bridegroom came;　10
and they that were ready went in with him to the
marriage: and the door was shut.

Afterward came also the other virgins, saying, Lord,　11
Lord, open to us.

But he answered and said, Verily I say unto you, I　12
know you not.

Watch therefore, for ye know neither the day nor　13
the hour wherein the Son of man cometh.

For the kingdom of heaven is as a man travelling　25:14
into a far country, who called his own servants, and
delivered unto them his goods.

And unto one he gave five talents, to another two,　15
and to another one; to every man according to his
several ability; and straightway took his journey.

Then he that had received the five talents went and traded with the same, and made them other five talents. 16

And likewise he that had received two, he also gained other two. 17

But he that had received one went and digged in the earth, and hid his lord's money. 18

After a long time the lord of those servants cometh, and reckoneth with them. 19

And so he that had received five talents came and brought other five talents, saying, Lord, thou deliveredst unto me five talents: behold, I have gained beside them five talents more. 20

His lord said unto him, Well done, thou good and faithful servant: thou hast been faithful over a few things, I will make thee ruler over many things: enter thou into the joy of thy lord. 21

He also that had received two talents came and said, Lord, thou deliveredst unto me two talents: behold, I have gained two other talents beside them. 22

His lord said unto him, Well done, good and faithful servant; thou hast been faithful over a few things, I will make thee ruler over many things: enter thou into the joy of thy lord. 23

Then he which had received the one talent came and said, Lord, I knew thee that thou art an hard man, reaping where thou hast not sown, and gathering where thou hast not strawed: 24

And I was afraid, and went and hid thy talent in the earth: lo, there thou hast that is thine. 25

His lord answered and said unto him, Thou wicked and slothful servant, thou knewest that I reap where I sowed not, and gather where I have not strawed: 26

Thou oughtest therefore to have put my money to the exchangers, and then at my coming I should have received mine own with usury.

27

Take therefore the talent from him, and give it unto him which hath ten talents.

28

For unto every one that hath shall be given, and he shall have abundance: but from him that hath not shall be taken away even that which he hath.

29

And cast ye the unprofitable servant into outer darkness: there shall be weeping and gnashing of teeth.

30

[Y]e have the poor always with you; but me ye have not always.

26:11

Take, eat; this is my body.

26:26

Drink ye all of it;

27

For this is my blood of the new testament, which is shed for many for the remission of sins.

28

But I say unto you, I will not drink henceforth of this fruit of the vine, until that day when I drink it new with you in my Father's kingdom.

29

...Hereafter shall ye see the Son of man sitting on the right hand of power, and coming in the clouds of heaven.

26:64

Be not afraid: go tell my brethren that they go into Galilee, and there shall they see me.

28:10

# The Gospel According to St. Mark

Come ye after me, and I will make you to become          1:17
fishers of men.

Son, thy sins be forgiven thee.          2: 5

Why reason ye these things in your hearts?          8

Whether is it easier to say to the sick of the palsy,          9
Thy sins be forgiven thee; or to say, Arise, and take
up thy bed, and walk?

But that ye may know that the Son of man hath          10
power on earth to forgive sins,

I say unto thee, Arise, and take up thy bed, and go          11
thy way into thine house.

They that are whole have no need of the physician,          2:17
but they that are sick: I came not to call the righteous, but sinners to repentance.

Daughter, thy faith hath made thee whole; go in          5:34
peace, and be whole of thy plague.

A prophet is not without honour, but in his own          6: 4
country, and among his own kin, and in his own
house.

Well hath Esaias prophesied of you hypocrites, as it          7: 6
is written, This people honoureth me with their lips,
but their heart is far from me.

Howbeit in vain do they worship me, teaching for doctrines the commandments of men.  7

For laying aside the commandment of God, ye hold the tradition of men, as the washing of pots and cups: and many other such like things ye do.  8

Full well ye reject the commandment of God, that ye may keep your own tradition.  9

For Moses said, Honour thy father and thy mother; and, Whoso curseth father or mother, let him die the death:  10

But ye say, If a man shall say to his father or mother, It is Corban, that is to say, a gift, by whatsoever thou mightest be profited by me; he shall be free.  11

And ye suffer him no more to do ought for his father or his mother;  12

Making the word of God of none effect through your tradition, which ye have delivered: and many such like things do ye.  13

Hearken unto me every one of you, and understand:  14

There is nothing from without a man, that entering into him can defile him: but the things which come out of him, those are they that defile the man.  15

If any man have ears to hear, let him hear.  16

Are ye so without understanding also? Do ye not perceive, that whatsoever thing from without entereth into the man, it cannot defile him;  18

Because it entereth not into his heart, but into the belly, and goeth out into the draught, purging all meats?  19

That which cometh out of the man, that defileth the man.  20

For from within, out of the heart of men, proceed evil thoughts, adulteries, fornications, murders,  21

Thefts, covetousness, wickedness, deceit, lasciviousness, an evil eye, blasphemy, pride, foolishness:  22

All these evil things come from within, and defile the man.  23

Ephphatha, *that is, Be opened.*  7:34

One thing thou lackest: go thy way, sell whatsoever thou hast, and give to the poor, and thou shalt have treasure in heaven: and come, take up the cross, and follow me.  10:21

[H]ow hard it is for them that trust in riches to enter into the kingdom of God!  24

For even the Son of man came not to be ministered unto, but to minister, and to give his life a ransom for many.  10:45

Is it not written, My house shall be called of all nations the house of prayer? but ye have made it a den of thieves.  11:17

Verily I say unto you, That this poor widow hath cast more in, than all they which have cast into the treasury:  12:43

For all they did cast in of their abundance; but she of her want did cast in all that she had, even all her living.  44

Verily I say unto thee, That this day, even in this night, before the cock crow twice, thou shalt deny me thrice.  14:30

# The Gospel According to St. Luke

It is written, That man shall not live by bread alone, but by every word of God.  4: 4

[E]xcept ye repent, ye shall all...perish.  13: 5

If any man come to me, and hate not his father, and mother, and wife, and children, and brethren, and sisters, yea, and his own life also, he cannot be my disciple.  14:26

There was in a city a judge, which feared not God, neither regarded man:  18: 2

And there was a widow in that city; and she came unto him, saying, Avenge me of mine adversary.  3

And he would not for a while: but afterward he said within himself, Though I fear not God, nor regard man;  4

Yet because this widow troubleth me, I will avenge her, lest by her continual coming she weary me.  5

Hear what the unjust judge saith.  6

And shall not God avenge his own elect, which cry day and night unto him, though he bear long with them?  7

I tell you that he will avenge them speedily. Nevertheless when the Son of man cometh, shall he find faith on the earth?  8

Suffer little children to come unto me, and forbid them not: for of such is the kingdom of God.  18:16

Verily I say unto you, Whosoever shall not receive the kingdom of God as a little child shall in no wise enter therein.  17

The children of this world marry, and are given in marriage:

20:34

But they which shall be accounted worthy to obtain that world, and the resurrection from the dead, neither marry, nor are given in marriage:

35

Neither can they die any more: for they are equal unto the angels; and are the children of God, being the children of the resurrection.

36

Now that the dead are raised, even Moses shewed at the bush, when he calleth the Lord the God of Abraham, and the God of Isaac, and the God of Jacob.

37

For he is not a God of the dead, but of the living: for all live unto him.

38

## The Gospel According to St. John

That which is born of the flesh is flesh; and that which is born of the Spirit is spirit.

3: 6

If I have told you earthly things, and ye believe not, how shall ye believe, if I tell you of heavenly things?

12

[T]hou hast had five husbands; and he whom thou now hast is not thy husband: in that saidst thou truly.

4:18

...Lift up your eyes, and look on the fields; for they are white already to harvest.

4:35

And he that reapeth receiveth wages, and gathereth fruit unto life eternal: that both he that soweth and he that reapeth may rejoice together.

36

And herein is that saying true, One soweth, and another reapeth. 37

I sent you to reap that whereon ye bestowed no labour: other men laboured, and ye are entered into their labours. 38

For the Father judgeth no man, but hath committed all judgment unto the Son: 5:22

That all men should honour the Son, even as they honour the Father. He that honoureth not the Son honoureth not the Father which hath sent him. 23

For had ye believed Moses, ye would have believed me: for he wrote of me. 5:46

But if ye believe not his writings, how shall ye believe my words? 47

And this is the Father's will which hath sent me, that of all which he hath given me I should lose nothing, but should raise it up again at the last day. 6:39

And this is the will of him that sent me, that every one which seeth the Son, and believeth on him, may have everlasting life: and I will raise him up at the last day. 40

I am that bread of life. 6:48

Your fathers did eat manna in the wilderness, and are dead. 49

This is the bread which cometh down from heaven, that a man may eat thereof, and not die. 50

I am the living bread which came down from heaven: if any man eat of this bread, he shall live for ever: and the bread that I will give is my flesh, which I will give for the life of the world. 51

Whoso eateth my flesh, and drinketh my blood, hath eternal life; and I will raise him up at the last day.  54

For my flesh is meat indeed, and my blood is drink indeed.  55

He that eateth my flesh, and drinketh my blood, dwelleth in me, and I in him.  56

The world cannot hate you; but me it hateth, because I testify of it, that the works thereof are evil.  7: 7

My doctrine is not mine, but his that sent me.  7:16

He that is without sin among you, let him first cast a stone at her.  8: 7

Ye are from beneath; I am from above: ye are of this world; I am not of this world.  8:23

And ye shall know the truth, and the truth shall make you free.  8:32

Verily, verily, I say unto you, If a man keep my saying, he shall never see death.  8:51

Verily, verily, I say unto you, Before Abraham was, I am.  8:58

I am the good shepherd: the good shepherd giveth his life for the sheep.  10:11

But he that is an hireling, and not the shepherd, whose own the sheep are not, seeth the wolf coming, and leaveth the sheep, and fleeth: and the wolf catcheth them, and scattereth the sheep.  12

The hireling fleeth, because he is an hireling, and careth not for the sheep. 13

I am the good shepherd, and know my sheep, and am known of mine. 14

As the Father knoweth me, even so know I the Father: and I lay down my life for the sheep. 15

And other sheep I have, which are not of this fold: them also I must bring, and they shall hear my voice; and there shall be one fold, and one shepherd. 16

Therefore doth my Father love me, because I lay down my life, that I might take it again. 17

No man taketh it from me, but I lay it down of myself. I have power to lay it down, and I have power to take it again. This commandment have I received of my Father. 18

I told you, and ye believed not: the works that I do in my Father's name, they bear witness of me. 25

But ye believe not, because ye are not of my sheep, as I said unto you. 26

My sheep hear my voice, and I know them, and they follow me: 27

And I give unto them eternal life; and they shall never perish, neither shall any man pluck them out of my hand. 28

My Father, which gave them me, is greater than all; and no man is able to pluck them out of my Father's hand. 29

I and my Father are one. 30

Many good works have I shewed you from my Father; for which of those works do ye stone me? 10:32

...If any man walk in the day, he stumbleth not, because he seeth the light of this world. 11: 9

But if a man walk in the night, he stumbleth, because there is no light in him. 10

Lazarus, come forth. 11:43

Loose him, and let him go. 44

And if any man hear my words, and believe not, I judge him not: for I came not to judge the world, but to save the world. 12:47

He that rejecteth me, and receiveth not my words, hath one that judgeth him: the word that I have spoken, the same shall judge him in the last day. 48

For I have not spoken of myself; but the Father which sent me, he gave me a commandment, what I should say, and what I should speak. 49

What I do thou knowest not now; but thou shalt know hereafter. 13: 7

Know ye what I have done to you? 13:12

Ye call me Master and Lord: and ye say well; for so I am. 13

If I then, your Lord and Master, have washed your feet; ye also ought to wash one another's feet. 14

Verily, verily, I say unto you, that one of you shall betray me. 13:21

Wilt thou lay down thy life for my sake? Verily, verily, I say unto thee, The cock shall not crow, till thou hast denied me thrice. 13:38

I am the way, the truth, and the life: no man cometh unto the Father, but by me.

14: 6

I will not leave you comfortless: I will come to you.

14:18

But the Comforter, which is the Holy Ghost, whom the Father will send in my name, he shall teach you all things, and bring all things to your remembrance, whatsoever I have said unto you.

14:26

Peace I leave with you, my peace I give unto you: not as the world giveth, give I unto you. Let not your heart be troubled, neither let it be afraid.

27

Abide in me, and I in you. As the branch cannot bear fruit of itself, except it abide in the vine; no more can ye, except ye abide in me.

15: 4

I am the vine, ye are the branches: He that abideth in me, and I in him, the same bringeth forth much fruit: for without me ye can do nothing.

5

This is my commandment, That ye love one another, as I have loved you.

15:12

Henceforth I call you not servants; for the servant knoweth not what his lord doeth: but I have called you friends; for all things that I have heard of my Father I have made known unto you.

15:15

A woman when she is in travail hath sorrow, because her hour is come: but as soon as she is delivered of the child, she remembereth no more the anguish, for joy that a man is born into the world.

16:21

And ye now therefore have sorrow: but I will see you again, and your heart shall rejoice, and your joy no man taketh from you. 22

For the Father himself loveth you, because ye have loved me, and have believed that I came out from God. 27

I came forth from the Father, and am come into the world: again, I leave the world, and go to the Father. 28

Put up thy sword into the sheath: the cup which my Father hath given me, shall I not drink it? 18:11

I spake openly to the world; I ever taught in the synagogue, and in the temple, whither the Jews always resort; and in secret have I said nothing. 20

Peace be unto you. 20:26

Reach hither thy finger, and behold my hands; and reach hither thy hand, and thrust it into my side: and be not faithless, but believing. 27

Thomas, because thou hast seen me, thou hast believed: blessed are they that have not seen, and yet have believed. 29

## The Acts of the Apostles

For John truly baptized with water; but ye shall be baptized with the Holy Ghost not many days hence. 1: 5

# PART III

# THE COMPLETE SAYINGS

## from the Four Gospels and the Acts of the Apostles

## in Chronological Order*

At the age of twelve Jesus disputes with scholars in the Temple.

Lk  2:49

How is it that ye sought me? wist ye not that I must be about my Father's business?

At about the age of thirty he is baptized in the River Jordan by John the Baptist.

Mt  3:15

Suffer it to be so now: for thus it becometh us to fulfil all righteousness.

After fasting forty days in the wilderness he is tempted by the Devil.

Mt  4: 4

It is written, Man shall not live by bread alone, but by every word that proceedeth out of the mouth of God.

It is written again, Thou shalt not tempt the Lord thy God.

7

___

* Insofar as chronology can be determined.

Get thee hence, Satan: for it is written, Thou shalt worship the Lord thy God, and him only shalt thou serve.

10

It is written, That man shall not live by bread alone, but by every word of God.

Lk 4: 4

Get thee behind me, Satan: for it is written, Thou shalt worship the Lord thy God, and him only shalt thou serve.

8

It is said, Thou shalt not tempt the Lord thy God.

12

He begins to preach the kingdom of God in Galilee.

Repent: for the kingdom of heaven is at hand.

Mt 4:17

The time is fulfilled, and the kingdom of God is at hand: repent ye, and believe the gospel.

Mk 1:15

He calls fishermen by the Sea of Galilee to fish for human catch.

Follow me, and I will make you fishers of men.

Mt 4:19

Come ye after me, and I will make you to become fishers of men.

Mk 1:17

Launch out into the deep, and let down your nets for a draught.

Lk 5: 4

Fear not; from henceforth thou shalt catch men.                    10

He calls five Galileans to follow him as disciples.

What seek ye?                                        Jn  1:38

Come and see.                                             39

Thou art Simon the son of Jona: thou          42
shalt be called Cephas, *which is by inter-*
*pretation, A stone.*

Follow me.                                               43

Behold an Israelite indeed, in whom is no        47
guile!

Before that Philip called thee, when thou        48
wast under the fig tree, I saw thee.

Because I said unto thee, I saw thee un-         50
der the fig tree, believest thou? thou shalt
see greater things than these.

Verily, verily, I say unto you, Hereafter ye     51
shall see heaven open, and the angels of
God ascending and descending upon the
Son of man.

He changes water into wine at a mar- riage feast in Cana of Galilee.

Woman, what have I to do with thee?        Jn  2: 4
mine hour is not yet come.

Fill the waterpots with water.                          7

Draw out now, and bear unto the gover-            8
nor of the feast.

Having gone up to Jerusalem for the Passover, he answers the question of Nicodemus, a learned Pharisee, about how to find the kingdom of God.

Verily, verily, I say unto thee, Except a man be born again, he cannot see the kingdom of God.

Jn 3: 3

Verily, verily, I say unto thee, Except a man be born of water and of the Spirit, he cannot enter into the kingdom of God.

5

That which is born of the flesh is flesh; and that which is born of the Spirit is spirit.

6

Marvel not that I said unto thee, Ye must be born again.

7

The wind bloweth where it listeth, and thou hearest the sound thereof, but canst not tell whence it cometh, and whither it goeth: so is every one that is born of the Spirit.

8

Art thou a master of Israel, and knowest not these things?

10

Verily, verily, I say unto thee, We speak that we do know, and testify that we have seen; and ye receive not our witness.

11

If I have told you earthly things, and ye believe not, how shall ye believe, if I tell you of heavenly things?

12

And no man hath ascended up to heaven, but he that came down from heaven, even the Son of man which is in heaven.  13

And as Moses lifted up the serpent in the wilderness, even so must the Son of man be lifted up:  14

That whosoever believeth in him should not perish, but have eternal life.  15

For God so loved the world, that he gave his only begotten Son, that whosoever believeth in him should not perish, but have everlasting life.  16

For God sent not his Son into the world to condemn the world; but that the world through him might be saved.  17

He that believeth on him is not condemned: but he that believeth not is condemned already, because he hath not believed in the name of the only begotten Son of God.  18

And this is the condemnation, that light is come into the world, and men loved darkness rather than light, because their deeds were evil.  19

For every one that doeth evil hateth the light, neither cometh to the light, lest his deeds should be reproved.  20

But he that doeth truth cometh to the light, that his deeds may be made manifest, that they are wrought in God.  21

Returning to Galilee
via Samaria, he
identifies himself to
a Samaritan
woman whom he
meets by chance at
Jacob's well.

Give me to drink.

Jn  4: 7

If thou knewest the gift of God, and who
it is that saith to thee, Give me to drink;
thou wouldest have asked of him, and he
would have given thee living water.

10

Whosoever drinketh of this water shall
thirst again:

13

But whosoever drinketh of the water that
I shall give him shall never thirst; but the
water that I shall give him shall be in him
a well of water springing up into everlasting life.

14

Go, call thy husband, and come hither.

16

Thou hast well said, I have no husband:

17

For thou hast had five husbands; and he
whom thou now hast is not thy husband:
in that saidst thou truly.

18

Woman, believe me, the hour cometh,
when ye shall neither in this mountain,
nor yet at Jerusalem, worship the Father.

21

Ye worship ye know not what: we know
what we worship: for salvation is of the
Jews.

22

But the hour cometh, and now is, when
the true worshippers shall worship the
Father in spirit and in truth: for the Father seeketh such to worship him.

23

God is a Spirit: and they that worship him must worship him in spirit and in truth.

24

I that speak unto thee am he.

26

Jesus teaches his disciples that their work is to reap what God has sowed.

I have meat to eat that ye know not of.

Jn 4:32

My meat is to do the will of him that sent me, and to finish his work.

34

Say not ye, There are yet four months, and then cometh harvest? behold, I say unto you, Lift up your eyes, and look on the fields; for they are white already to harvest.

35

And he that reapeth receiveth wages, and gathereth fruit unto life eternal: that both he that soweth and he that reapeth may rejoice together.

36

And herein is that saying true, One soweth, and another reapeth.

37

I sent you to reap that whereon ye bestowed no labour: other men laboured, and ye are entered into their labours.

38

As he journeys from town to town in Galilee, preaching in the synagogues, Jesus casts an unclean spirit out of a man.

Hold thy peace, and come out of him.

Mk 1:25

Let us go into the next towns, that I may preach there also: for therefore came I forth.

38

Hold thy peace, and come out of him.

Lk 4:35

I must preach the kingdom of God to other cities also: for therefore am I sent.

43

He heals a nobleman's son.

Except ye see signs and wonders, ye will not believe.

Jn 4:48

Go thy way; thy son liveth.

50

Having gone up to Jerusalem for another feast, Jesus heals a cripple on the Sabbath at the Pool of Bethesda.

Wilt thou be made whole?

Jn 5: 6

Rise, take up thy bed, and walk.

8

Behold, thou art made whole: sin no more, lest a worse thing come unto thee.

14

His work of healing is no breach of the Sabbath because it is the work of God, his Father.

My Father worketh hitherto, and I work.

Jn 5:17

Verily, verily, I say unto you, The Son can do nothing of himself, but what he seeth the Father do: for what things soever he doeth, these also doeth the Son likewise.

19

For the Father loveth the Son, and sheweth him all things that himself doeth: and he will shew him greater works than these, that ye may marvel.

20

For as the Father raiseth up the dead, and quickeneth them; even so the Son quickeneth whom he will.

21

For the Father judgeth no man, but hath committed all judgment unto the Son:

22

That all men should honour the Son, even as they honour the Father. He that honoureth not the Son honoureth not the Father which hath sent him.

23

Verily, verily, I say unto you, He that heareth my word, and believeth on him that sent me, hath everlasting life, and shall not come into condemnation; but is passed from death unto life.

24

Verily, verily, I say unto you, The hour is coming, and now is, when the dead shall hear the voice of the Son of God: and they that hear shall live.

25

For as the Father hath life in himself; so hath he given to the Son to have life in himself;

26

And hath given him authority to execute judgment also, because he is the Son of man.

27

Marvel not at this: for the hour is coming, in the which all that are in the graves shall hear his voice,

28

And shall come forth; they that have done 29
good, unto the resurrection of life; and
they that have done evil, unto the resurrection of damnation.

I can of mine own self do nothing: as I 30
hear, I judge: and my judgment is just;
because I seek not mine own will, but the
will of the Father which hath sent me.

If I bear witness of myself, my witness is 31
not true.

There is another that beareth witness of 32
me; and I know that the witness which
he witnesseth of me is true.

Ye sent unto John, and he bare witness 33
unto the truth.

But I receive not testimony from man: 34
but these things I say, that ye might be
saved.

He was a burning and a shining light: and 35
ye were willing for a season to rejoice in
his light.

But I have greater witness than that of 36
John: for the works which the Father hath
given me to finish, the same works that I
do, bear witness of me, that the Father
hath sent me.

And the Father himself, which hath sent 37
me, hath borne witness of me. Ye have
neither heard his voice at any time, nor
seen his shape.

And ye have not his word abiding in you: 38
for whom he hath sent, him ye believe not.

Search the scriptures; for in them ye think
ye have eternal life: and they are they
which testify of me.

39

And ye will not come to me, that ye might
have life.

40

I receive not honour from men.

41

But I know you, that ye have not the love
of God in you.

42

I am come in my Father's name, and ye
receive me not: if another shall come in
his own name, him ye will receive.

43

How can ye believe, which receive honour
one of another, and seek not the honour
that cometh from God only?

44

Do not think that I will accuse you to the
Father: there is one that accuseth you, even
Moses, in whom ye trust.

45

For had ye believed Moses, ye would have
believed me: for he wrote of me.

46

But if ye believe not his writings, how shall
ye believe my words?

47

Once again in Galilee, Jesus preaches to the multitude a sermon best known as "the sermon on the mount."

Blessed are the poor in spirit: for theirs is
the kingdom of heaven.

Mt 5: 3

Blessed are they that mourn: for they shall
be comforted.

4

Blessed are the meek: for they shall in-
herit the earth.                                         5

Blessed are they which do hunger and          6
thirst after righteousness: for they shall be
filled.

Blessed are the merciful: for they shall       7
obtain mercy.

Blessed are the pure in heart: for they shall   8
see God.

Blessed are the peacemakers: for they shall     9
be called the children of God.

Blessed are they which are persecuted for      10
righteousness' sake: for theirs is the kingdom of heaven.

Blessed are ye, when men shall revile you,      11
and persecute you, and shall say all manner of evil against you falsely, for my sake.

Rejoice, and be exceeding glad: for great       12
is your reward in heaven: for so persecuted
they the prophets which were before you.

Ye are the salt of the earth: but if the salt   13
have lost his savour, wherewith shall it be
salted? it is thenceforth good for nothing,
but to be cast out, and to be trodden under foot of men.

Ye are the light of the world. A city that is   14
set on an hill cannot be hid.

Neither do men light a candle, and put it       15
under a bushel, but on a candlestick; and
it giveth light unto all that are in the
house.

*Related Saying\**

No man, when he hath lighted a candle,
putteth it in a secret place, neither under
a bushel, but on a candlestick, that they
which come in may see the light.

Lk 11:33

Mt 5 [continued]
16

Let your light so shine before men, that
they may see your good works, and glorify your Father which is in heaven.

Think not that I am come to destroy the
law, or the prophets: I am not come to
destroy, but to fulfil.

17

For verily I say unto you, Till heaven and
earth pass, one jot or one tittle shall in no
wise pass from the law, till all be fulfilled.

18

*Related Saying*

And it is easier for heaven and earth to
pass, than one tittle of the law to fail.

Lk 16:17

Mt 5 [continued]
19

Whosoever therefore shall break one of
these least commandments, and shall
teach men so, he shall be called the least
in the kingdom of heaven: but whosoever
shall do and teach them, the same shall
be called great in the kingdom of heaven.

For I say unto you, That except your righteousness shall exceed the righteousness

20

---

*\* The annotation "Related Saying" or "Related Sayings" means that these words,
although similar to the ones above them, are spoken at a different time or to a different person.*

of the scribes and Pharisees, ye shall in no case enter into the kingdom of heaven.

Ye have heard that it was said by them of old time, Thou shalt not kill; and whosoever shall kill shall be in danger of the judgment:                              21

But I say unto you, That whosoever is angry with his brother without a cause shall be in danger of the judgment: and whosoever shall say to his brother, Raca, shall be in danger of the council: but whosoever shall say, Thou fool, shall be in danger of hell fire.                              22

Therefore if thou bring thy gift to the altar, and there rememberest that thy brother hath ought against thee;                              23

Leave there thy gift before the altar, and go thy way; first be reconciled to thy brother, and then come and offer thy gift.                              24

Agree with thine adversary quickly, whiles thou art in the way with him; lest at any time the adversary deliver thee to the judge, and the judge deliver thee to the officer, and thou be cast into prison.                              25

Verily I say unto thee, Thou shalt by no means come out thence, till thou hast paid the uttermost farthing.                              26

### Related Saying

Yea, and why even of yourselves judge ye not what is right?                              Lk 12:57

When thou goest with thine adversary to the magistrate, as thou art in the way, give                              58 diligence that thou mayest be delivered from him; lest he hale thee to the judge, and the judge deliver thee to the officer, and the officer cast thee into prison.

I tell thee, thou shalt not depart thence, till thou hast paid the very last mite.

59

Mt 5 [continued]

Ye have heard that it was said by them of old time, Thou shalt not commit adultery:

27

But I say unto you, That whosoever looketh on a woman to lust after her hath committed adultery with her already in his heart.

28

And if thy right eye offend thee, pluck it out, and cast it from thee: for it is profitable for thee that one of thy members should perish, and not that thy whole body should be cast into hell.

29

And if thy right hand offend thee, cut it off, and cast it from thee: for it is profitable for thee that one of thy members should perish, and not that thy whole body should be cast into hell.

30

It hath been said, Whosoever shall put away his wife, let him give her a writing of divorcement:

31

But I say unto you, That whosoever shall put away his wife, saving for the cause of fornication, causeth her to commit adultery: and whosoever shall marry her that is divorced committeth adultery.

32

*Related Saying*

Whosoever putteth away his wife, and       Lk 16:18
marrieth another, committeth adultery:
and whosoever marrieth her that is put
away from her husband committeth adultery.


                                            Mt 5 [continued]
Again, ye have heard that it hath been said       33
by them of old time, Thou shalt not forswear thyself, but shalt perform unto the
Lord thine oaths:

But I say unto you, Swear not at all; nei-       34
ther by heaven; for it is God's throne:

Nor by the earth; for it is his footstool:       35
neither by Jerusalem; for it is the city of
the great King.

Neither shalt thou swear by thy head, be-       36
cause thou canst not make one hair white
or black.

But let your communication be, Yea, yea;       37
Nay, nay: for whatsoever is more than
these cometh of evil.

Ye have heard that it hath been said, An       38
eye for an eye, and a tooth for a tooth:

But I say unto you, That ye resist not evil:       39
but whosoever shall smite thee on thy
right cheek, turn to him the other also.

And if any man will sue thee at the law,       40
and take away thy coat, let him have thy
cloke also.

And whosoever shall compel thee to go a mile, go with him twain. 41

Give to him that asketh thee, and from him that would borrow of thee turn not thou away. 42

Ye have heard that it hath been said, Thou shalt love thy neighbour, and hate thine enemy. 43

But I say unto you, Love your enemies, bless them that curse you, do good to them that hate you, and pray for them which despitefully use you, and persecute you; 44

That ye may be the children of your Father which is in heaven: for he maketh his sun to rise on the evil and on the good, and sendeth rain on the just and on the unjust. 45

For if ye love them which love you, what reward have ye? do not even the publicans the same? 46

And if ye salute your brethren only, what do ye more than others? do not even the publicans so? 47

Be ye therefore perfect, even as your Father which is in heaven is perfect. 48

Take heed that ye do not your alms before men, to be seen of them: otherwise ye have no reward of your Father which is in heaven. Mt 6: 1

Therefore when thou doest thine alms, do not sound a trumpet before thee, as the hypocrites do in the synagogues and in the streets, that they may have glory of men. Verily I say unto you, They have their reward. 2

But when thou doest alms, let not thy left hand know what thy right hand doeth: 3

That thine alms may be in secret: and thy Father which seeth in secret himself shall reward thee openly. 4

And when thou prayest, thou shalt not be as the hypocrites are: for they love to pray standing in the synagogues and in the corners of the streets, that they may be seen of men. Verily I say unto you, They have their reward. 5

But thou, when thou prayest, enter into thy closet, and when thou hast shut thy door, pray to thy Father which is in secret; and thy Father which seeth in secret shall reward thee openly. 6

But when ye pray, use not vain repetitions, as the heathen do: for they think that they shall be heard for their much speaking. 7

Be not ye therefore like unto them: for your Father knoweth what things ye have need of, before ye ask him. 8

After this manner therefore pray ye: Our Father which art in heaven, Hallowed be thy name. 9

Thy kingdom come. Thy will be done in earth, as it is in heaven.

10

Give us this day our daily bread.

11

And forgive us our debts, as we forgive our debtors.

12

And lead us not into temptation, but deliver us from evil: For thine is the kingdom, and the power, and the glory, for ever. Amen.

13

### Related Saying

When ye pray, say, Our Father which art in heaven, Hallowed be thy name. Thy kingdom come. Thy will be done, as in heaven, so in earth.

Lk 11: 2

Give us day by day our daily bread.

3

And forgive us our sins; for we also forgive every one that is indebted to us. And lead us not into temptation; but deliver us from evil.

4

Mt 6 [continued]

For if ye forgive men their trespasses, your heavenly Father will also forgive you:

14

But if ye forgive not men their trespasses, neither will your Father forgive your trespasses.

15

Moreover when ye fast, be not, as the hypocrites, of a sad countenance: for they disfigure their faces, that they may appear unto men to fast. Verily I say unto you, They have their reward.

16

But thou, when thou fastest, anoint thine head, and wash thy face;    17

That thou appear not unto men to fast, but unto thy Father which is in secret: and thy Father, which seeth in secret, shall reward thee openly.    18

Lay not up for yourselves treasures upon earth, where moth and rust doth corrupt, and where thieves break through and steal:    19

But lay up for yourselves treasures in heaven, where neither moth nor rust doth corrupt, and where thieves do not break through nor steal:    20

For where your treasure is, there will your heart be also.    21

### Related Saying

Sell that ye have, and give alms; provide yourselves bags which wax not old, a treasure in the heavens that faileth not, where no thief approacheth, neither moth corrupteth.    Lk 12:33

For where your treasure is, there will your heart be also.    34

Mt 6 [continued]

The light of the body is the eye: if therefore thine eye be single, thy whole body shall be full of light.    22

But if thine eye be evil, thy whole body shall be full of darkness. If therefore the light that is in thee be darkness, how great is that darkness!    23

*Related Saying*

The light of the body is the eye: therefore
when thine eye is single, thy whole body
also is full of light; but when thine eye is
evil, thy body also is full of darkness.

Lk 11:34

Take heed therefore that the light which
is in thee be not darkness.

35

If thy whole body therefore be full of light,
having no part dark, the whole shall be
full of light, as when the bright shining
of a candle doth give thee light.

36

Mt 6 [continued]

No man can serve two masters: for either
he will hate the one, and love the other;
or else he will hold to the one, and despise the other. Ye cannot serve God and
mammon.

24

Therefore I say unto you, Take no thought
for your life, what ye shall eat, or what ye
shall drink; nor yet for your body, what
ye shall put on. Is not the life more than
meat, and the body than raiment?

25

Behold the fowls of the air: for they sow
not, neither do they reap, nor gather into
barns; yet your heavenly Father feedeth
them. Are ye not much better than they?

26

Which of you by taking thought can add
one cubit unto his stature?

27

And why take ye thought for raiment?
Consider the lilies of the field, how they
grow; they toil not, neither do they spin:

28

And yet I say unto you, That even Solomon in all his glory was not arrayed like one of these.

29

Wherefore, if God so clothe the grass of the field, which to day is, and to morrow is cast into the oven, shall he not much more clothe you, O ye of little faith?

30

Therefore take no thought, saying, What shall we eat? or, What shall we drink? or, Wherewithal shall we be clothed?

31

(For after all these things do the Gentiles seek:) for your heavenly Father knoweth that ye have need of all these things.

32

But seek ye first the kingdom of God, and his righteousness; and all these things shall be added unto you.

33

### Related Saying

Therefore I say unto you, Take no thought for your life, what ye shall eat; neither for the body, what ye shall put on.

Lk 12:22

The life is more than meat, and the body is more than raiment.

23

Consider the ravens: for they neither sow nor reap; which neither have storehouse nor barn; and God feedeth them: how much more are ye better than the fowls?

24

And which of you with taking thought can add to his stature one cubit?

25

If ye then be not able to do that thing which is least, why take ye thought for the rest?

26

Consider the lilies how they grow: they toil not, they spin not; and yet I say unto you, that Solomon in all his glory was not arrayed like one of these.

27

If then God so clothe the grass, which is to day in the field, and to morrow is cast into the oven; how much more will he clothe you, O ye of little faith?

28

And seek not ye what ye shall eat, or what ye shall drink, neither be ye of doubtful mind.

29

For all these things do the nations of the world seek after: and your Father knoweth that ye have need of these things.

30

But rather seek ye the kingdom of God; and all these things shall be added unto you.

31

Fear not, little flock; for it is your Father's good pleasure to give you the kingdom.

32

Mt 6 [continued]

Take therefore no thought for the morrow: for the morrow shall take thought for the things of itself. Sufficient unto the day is the evil thereof.

34

Judge not, that ye be not judged.

Mt 7: 1

For with what judgment ye judge, ye shall be judged: and with what measure ye mete, it shall be measured to you again.

2

And why beholdest thou the mote that is in thy brother's eye, but considerest not the beam that is in thine own eye?

3

Or how wilt thou say to thy brother, Let me pull out the mote out of thine eye; and, behold, a beam is in thine own eye?
4

Thou hypocrite, first cast out the beam out of thine own eye; and then shalt thou see clearly to cast out the mote out of thy brother's eye.
5

Give not that which is holy unto the dogs, neither cast ye your pearls before swine, lest they trample them under their feet, and turn again and rend you.
6

Ask, and it shall be given you; seek, and ye shall find; knock, and it shall be opened unto you:
7

For every one that asketh receiveth; and he that seeketh findeth; and to him that knocketh it shall be opened.
8

### Related Saying

Which of you shall have a friend, and shall go unto him at midnight, and say unto him, Friend, lend me three loaves;
Lk 11: 5

For a friend of mine in his journey is come to me, and I have nothing to set before him?
6

And he from within shall answer and say, Trouble me not: the door is now shut, and my children are with me in bed; I cannot rise and give thee.
7

I say unto you, Though he will not rise and give him, because he is his friend, yet because of his importunity he will rise and give him as many as he needeth.
8

And I say unto you, Ask, and it shall be given you; seek, and ye shall find; knock, and it shall be opened unto you.

9

For every one that asketh receiveth; and he that seeketh findeth; and to him that knocketh it shall be opened.

10

Mt 7 [continued]

Or what man is there of you, whom if his son ask bread, will he give him a stone?

9

Or if he ask a fish, will he give him a serpent?

10

If ye then, being evil, know how to give good gifts unto your children, how much more shall your Father which is in heaven give good things to them that ask him?

11

*Related Saying*

If a son shall ask bread of any of you that is a father, will he give him a stone? or if he ask a fish, will he for a fish give him a serpent?

Lk 11: 11

Or if he shall ask an egg, will he offer him a scorpion?

12

If ye then, being evil, know how to give good gifts unto your children: how much more shall your heavenly Father give the Holy Spirit to them that ask him?

13

Mt 7 [continued]

Therefore all things whatsoever ye would that men should do to you, do ye even so to them: for this is the law and the prophets.

12

Enter ye in at the strait gate: for wide is the gate, and broad is the way, that leadeth to destruction, and many there be which go in thereat:

13

Because strait is the gate, and narrow is the way, which leadeth unto life, and few there be that find it.

14

*Related Saying*

Strive to enter in at the strait gate: for many, I say unto you, will seek to enter in, and shall not be able.

Lk 13:24

Mt 7 [continued]

Beware of false prophets, which come to you in sheep's clothing, but inwardly they are ravening wolves.

15

Ye shall know them by their fruits. Do men gather grapes of thorns, or figs of thistles?

16

Even so every good tree bringeth forth good fruit; but a corrupt tree bringeth forth evil fruit.

17

A good tree cannot bring forth evil fruit, neither can a corrupt tree bring forth good fruit.

18

Every tree that bringeth not forth good fruit is hewn down, and cast into the fire.

19

Wherefore by their fruits ye shall know them.

20

Not every one that saith unto me, Lord, Lord, shall enter into the kingdom of heaven; but he that doeth the will of my Father which is in heaven.

21

Many will say to me in that day, Lord, Lord, have we not prophesied in thy name? and in thy name have cast out devils? and in thy name done many wonderful works?

22

And then will I profess unto them, I never knew you: depart from me, ye that work iniquity.

23

### Related Saying

Then shall ye begin to say, We have eaten and drunk in thy presence, and thou hast taught in our streets.

Lk 13:26

But he shall say, I tell you, I know you not whence ye are; depart from me, all ye workers of iniquity.

27

Mt 7 [continued]

Therefore whosoever heareth these sayings of mine, and doeth them, I will liken him unto a wise man, which built his house upon a rock:

24

And the rain descended, and the floods came, and the winds blew, and beat upon that house; and it fell not: for it was founded upon a rock.

25

And every one that heareth these sayings of mine, and doeth them not, shall be likened unto a foolish man, which built his house upon the sand:

26

And the rain descended, and the floods came, and the winds blew, and beat upon that house; and it fell: and great was the fall of it.

27

Blessed be ye poor: for yours is the kingdom of God.

Lk 6:20

Blessed are ye that hunger now: for ye shall be filled. Blessed are ye that weep now: for ye shall laugh.

21

Blessed are ye, when men shall hate you, and when they shall separate you from their company, and shall reproach you, and cast out your name as evil, for the Son of man's sake.

22

Rejoice ye in that day, and leap for joy: for, behold, your reward is great in heaven: for in the like manner did their fathers unto the prophets.

23

But woe unto you that are rich! for ye have received your consolation.

24

Woe unto you that are full! for ye shall hunger. Woe unto you that laugh now! for ye shall mourn and weep.

25

Woe unto you, when all men shall speak well of you! for so did their fathers to the false prophets.

26

But I say unto you which hear, Love your enemies, do good to them which hate you,

27

Bless them that curse you, and pray for them which despitefully use you.

28

And unto him that smiteth thee on the one cheek offer also the other; and him that taketh away thy cloke forbid not to take thy coat also.

29

Give to every man that asketh of thee; and of him that taketh away thy goods ask them not again.

30

And as ye would that men should do to you, do ye also to them likewise. 31

For if ye love them which love you, what thank have ye? for sinners also love those that love them. 32

And if ye do good to them which do good to you, what thank have ye? for sinners also do even the same. 33

And if ye lend to them of whom ye hope to receive, what thank have ye? for sinners also lend to sinners, to receive as much again. 34

But love ye your enemies, and do good, and lend, hoping for nothing again; and your reward shall be great, and ye shall be the children of the Highest: for he is kind unto the unthankful and to the evil. 35

Be ye therefore merciful, as your Father also is merciful. 36

Judge not, and ye shall not be judged: condemn not, and ye shall not be condemned: forgive, and ye shall be forgiven: 37

Give, and it shall be given unto you; good measure, pressed down, and shaken together, and running over, shall men give into your bosom. For with the same measure that ye mete withal it shall be measured to you again. 38

Can the blind lead the blind? shall they not both fall into the ditch? 39

The disciple is not above his master: but every one that is perfect shall be as his master. 40

And why beholdest thou the mote that is
in thy brother's eye, but perceivest not the
beam that is in thine own eye?

41

Either how canst thou say to thy brother,
Brother, let me pull out the mote that is
in thine eye, when thou thyself beholdest
not the beam that is in thine own eye?
Thou hypocrite, cast out first the beam
out of thine own eye, and then shalt thou
see clearly to pull out the mote that is in
thy brother's eye.

42

For a good tree bringeth not forth corrupt fruit; neither doth a corrupt tree
bring forth good fruit.

43

For every tree is known by his own fruit.
For of thorns men do not gather figs, nor
of a bramble bush gather they grapes.

44

A good man out of the good treasure of
his heart bringeth forth that which is
good; and an evil man out of the evil treasure of his heart bringeth forth that which
is evil: for of the abundance of the heart
his mouth speaketh.

45

And why call ye me, Lord, Lord, and do
not the things which I say?

46

Whosoever cometh to me, and heareth my
sayings, and doeth them, I will shew you
to whom he is like:

47

He is like a man which built an house,
and digged deep, and laid the foundation
on a rock: and when the flood arose, the
stream beat vehemently upon that house,
and could not shake it: for it was founded
upon a rock.

48

But he that heareth, and doeth not, is like a man that without a foundation built an house upon the earth; against which the stream did beat vehemently, and immediately it fell; and the ruin of that house was great.

49

Jesus heals a leper.

I will; be thou clean.

Mt 8: 3

See thou tell no man; but go thy way, shew thyself to the priest, and offer the gift that Moses commanded, for a testimony unto them.

4

I will; be thou clean.

Mk 1:41

See thou say nothing to any man: but go thy way, shew thyself to the priest, and offer for thy cleansing those things which Moses commanded, for a testimony unto them.

44

I will: be thou clean.

Lk 5:13

[T]ell no man: but go, and shew thyself to the priest, and offer for thy cleansing, according as Moses commanded, for a testimony unto them.

14

Jesus heals a centurion's (i.e. a Gentile's) servant.

I will come and heal him.

Mt 8: 7

Verily I say unto you, I have not found so great faith, no, not in Israel.

10

And I say unto you, That many shall come from the east and west, and shall sit down with Abraham, and Isaac, and Jacob, in the kingdom of heaven.

11

But the children of the kingdom shall be cast out into outer darkness: there shall be weeping and gnashing of teeth.

12

### Related Saying

There shall be weeping and gnashing of teeth, when ye shall see Abraham, and Isaac, and Jacob, and all the prophets, in the kingdom of God, and you yourselves thrust out.

Lk 13:28

And they shall come from the east, and from the west, and from the north, and from the south, and shall sit down in the kingdom of God.

29

And, behold, there are last which shall be first, and there are first which shall be last.

30

Mt 8 [continued]

Go thy way; and as thou hast believed, so be it done unto thee.

13

I say unto you, I have not found so great faith, no, not in Israel.

Lk 7: 9

Jesus raises a widow's son.

Weep not.

Lk 7:13

Young man, I say unto thee, Arise.

14

Jesus forgives a paralytic his sins and only afterwards heals his paralysis ("palsy"), causing the Pharisees to suspect him of blasphemy and the multitude to glorify God.

Son, be of good cheer; thy sins be forgiven thee.

Mt 9: 2

Wherefore think ye evil in your hearts?

4

For whether is easier, to say, Thy sins be forgiven thee; or to say, Arise, and walk?

5

But that ye may know that the Son of man hath power on earth to forgive sins, *(then saith he to the sick of the palsy,)* Arise, take up thy bed, and go unto thine house.

6

Son, thy sins be forgiven thee.

Mk 2: 5

Why reason ye these things in your hearts?

8

Whether is it easier to say to the sick of the palsy, Thy sins be forgiven thee; or to say, Arise, and take up thy bed, and walk?

9

But that ye may know that the Son of man hath power on earth to forgive sins, *(he saith to the sick of the palsy,)*

10

I say unto thee, Arise, and take up thy bed, and go thy way into thine house.

11

Man, thy sins are forgiven thee.

Lk 5:20

What reason ye in your hearts?

22

Whether is easier, to say, Thy sins be for-given thee; or to say, Rise up and walk?

23

But that ye may know that the Son of man hath power upon earth to forgive sins, *(he saith to the sick of the palsy,)* I say unto thee, Arise, and take up thy couch, and go into thine house.

24

Jesus calls Levi or Matthew and, hav-ing dined with publicans and sin-ners at his house, justifies himself to the Pharisees and tells them why his disciples do not fast as John the Baptist's do.

Follow me.

Mt 9: 9

They that be whole need not a physician, but they that are sick.

12

But go ye and learn what that meaneth, I will have mercy, and not sacrifice: for I am not come to call the righteous, but sinners to repentence.

13

Can the children of the bridechamber mourn, as long as the bridegroom is with them? but the days will come, when the bridegroom shall be taken from them, and then shall they fast.

15

No man putteth a piece of new cloth unto an old garment, for that which is put in to fill it up taketh from the garment, and the rent is made worse.

16

Neither do men put new wine into old
bottles: else the bottles break, and the wine
runneth out, and the bottles perish: but
they put new wine into new bottles, and
both are preserved.

17

Follow me.

Mk 2:14

They that are whole have no need of the
physician, but they that are sick: I came
not to call the righteous, but sinners to
repentance.

17

Can the children of the bridechamber fast,
while the bridegroom is with them? as
long as they have the bridegroom with
them, they cannot fast.

19

But the days will come, when the bridegroom shall be taken away from them, and
then shall they fast in those days.

20

No man also seweth a piece of new cloth
on an old garment: else the new piece that
filled it up taketh away from the old, and
the rent is made worse.

21

And no man putteth new wine into old
bottles: else the new wine doth burst the
bottles, and the wine is spilled, and the
bottles will be marred: but new wine must
be put into new bottles.

22

Follow me.

Lk 5:27

They that are whole need not a physician;
but they that are sick.

31

I came not to call the righteous, but sinners to repentance.

32

Can ye make the children of the bridechamber fast, while the bridegroom is with them?

34

But the days will come, when the bridegroom shall be taken away from them, and then shall they fast in those days.

35

No man putteth a piece of a new garment upon an old; if otherwise, then both the new maketh a rent, and the piece that was taken out of the new agreeth not with the old.

36

And no man putteth new wine into old bottles; else the new wine will burst the bottles, and be spilled, and the bottles shall perish.

37

But new wine must be put into new bottles; and both are preserved.

38

No man also having drunk old wine straightway desireth new: for he saith, The old is better.

39

Jesus justifies himself to the Pharisees for plucking ears of grain ("corn") and healing a man with a withered hand on the Sabbath.

Have ye not read what David did, when he was an hungred, and they that were with him;

Mt 12: 3

How he entered into the house of God, and did eat the shewbread, which was not lawful for him to eat, neither for them

4

which were with him, but only for the priests?

Or have ye not read in the law, how that on the sabbath days the priests in the temple profane the sabbath, and are blameless?

5

But I say unto you, That in this place is one greater than the temple.

6

But if ye had known what this meaneth, I will have mercy, and not sacrifice, ye would not have condemned the guiltless.

7

For the Son of man is Lord even of the sabbath day.

8

What man shall there be among you, that shall have one sheep, and if it fall into a pit on the sabbath day, will he not lay hold on it, and lift it out?

11

How much then is a man better than a sheep? Wherefore it is lawful to do well on the sabbath days.

12

Stretch forth thine hand.

13

Have ye never read what David did, when he had need, and was an hungred, he, and they that were with him?

Mk 2:25

How he went into the house of God in the days of Abiathar the high priest, and did eat the shewbread, which is not lawful to eat but for the priests, and gave also to them which were with him?

26

The sabbath was made for man, and not man for the sabbath:

27

Therefore the Son of man is Lord also of the sabbath.

28

Stand forth.

Mk 3: 3

Is it lawful to do good on the sabbath days, or to do evil? to save life, or to kill?

4

Stretch forth thine hand.

5

Have ye not read so much as this, what David did, when himself was an hungred, and they which were with him;

Lk 6: 3

How he went into the house of God, and did take and eat the shewbread, and gave also to them that were with him; which it is not lawful to eat but for the priests alone?

4

That the Son of man is Lord also of the sabbath.

5

Rise up, and stand forth in the midst.

8

I will ask you one thing; Is it lawful on the sabbath days to do good, or to do evil? to save life, or to destroy it?

9

Stretch forth thy hand.

10

Jesus is moved with compassion by the sight of the multitude, who are like lost sheep.

The harvest truly is plenteous, but the labourers are few;

Mt 9:37

Pray ye therefore the Lord of the harvest, that he will send forth labourers into his harvest.

38

### Related Saying

The harvest truly is great, but the labourers are few: pray ye therefore the Lord of the harvest, that he would send forth labourers into his harvest.

Lk 10: 2

Jesus empowers twelve disciples to do his work and sends them forth.

Go not into the way of the Gentiles, and into any city of the Samaritans enter ye not:

Mt 10: 5

But go rather to the lost sheep of the house of Israel.

6

And as ye go, preach, saying, The kingdom of heaven is at hand.

7

Heal the sick, cleanse the lepers, raise the dead, cast out devils: freely ye have received, freely give.

8

Provide neither gold, nor silver, nor brass in your purses,

9

Nor scrip for your journey, neither two coats, neither shoes, nor yet staves: for the workman is worthy of his meat.

10

And into whatsoever city or town ye shall enter, enquire who in it is worthy; and there abide till ye go thence.

11

And when ye come into an house, salute it.                                    12

And if the house be worthy, let your peace come upon it: but if it be not worthy, let your peace return to you.                                    13

And whosoever shall not receive you, nor hear your words, when ye depart out of that house or city, shake off the dust of your feet.                                    14

Verily I say unto you, It shall be more tolerable for the land of Sodom and Gomorrha in the day of judgment, than for that city.                                    15

Behold, I send you forth as sheep in the midst of wolves: be ye therefore wise as serpents, and harmless as doves.                                    16

In what place soever ye enter into an house, there abide till ye depart from that place.                                    Mk 6:10

And whosoever shall not receive you, nor hear you, when ye depart thence, shake off the dust under your feet for a testimony against them. Verily I say unto you, It shall be more tolerable for Sodom and Gomorrha in the day of judgment, than for that city.                                    11

Take nothing for your journey, neither staves, nor scrip, neither bread, neither money; neither have two coats apiece.                                    Lk 9: 3

And whatsoever house ye enter into, there abide, and thence depart.                                    4

And whosoever will not receive you, when            5
ye go out of that city, shake off the very
dust from your feet for a testimony against
them.

## Related Saying

Go your ways: behold, I send you forth        Lk 10: 3
as lambs among wolves.

Carry neither purse, nor scrip, nor shoes:            4
and salute no man by the way.

And into whatsoever house ye enter, first            5
say, Peace be to this house.

And if the son of peace be there, your            6
peace shall rest upon it: if not, it shall turn
to you again.

And in the same house remain, eating and            7
drinking such things as they give: for the
labourer is worthy of his hire. Go not from
house to house.

And into whatsoever city ye enter, and            8
they receive you, eat such things as are set
before you:

And heal the sick that are therein, and say            9
unto them, The kingdom of God is come
nigh unto you.

But into whatsoever city ye enter, and they            10
receive you not, go your ways out into the
streets of the same, and say,

Even the very dust of your city, which            11
cleaveth on us, we do wipe off against you:
notwithstanding be ye sure of this, that
the kingdom of God is come nigh unto
you.

But I say unto you, that it shall be more tolerable in that day for Sodom, than for that city.

12

Jesus foresees that his disciples will suffer persecution.

But beware of men: for they will deliver you up to the councils, and they will scourge you in their synagogues;

Mt 10:17

And ye shall be brought before governors and kings for my sake, for a testimony against them and the Gentiles.

18

But when they deliver you up, take no thought how or what ye shall speak: for it shall be given you in that same hour what ye shall speak.

19

For it is not ye that speak, but the Spirit of your Father which speaketh in you.

20

*Related Saying*
And when they bring you unto the synagogues, and unto magistrates, and powers, take ye no thought how or what thing ye shall answer, or what ye shall say:

Lk 12:11

For the Holy Ghost shall teach you in the same hour what ye ought to say.

12

Mt 10 [continued]

And the brother shall deliver up the brother to death, and the father the child: and the children shall rise up against their parents, and cause them to be put to death.

21

And ye shall be hated of all men for my name's sake: but he that endureth to the end shall be saved.

22

But when they persecute you in this city, flee ye into another: for verily I say unto you, Ye shall not have gone over the cities of Israel, till the Son of man be come.

23

The disciple is not above his master, nor the servant above his lord.

24

It is enough for the disciple that he be as his master, and the servant as his lord. If they have called the master of the house Beelzebub, how much more shall they call them of his household?

25

Fear them not therefore....

26

He urges them to confess their faith without fear.

Mt 10:26

[F]or there is nothing covered, that shall not be revealed; and hid, that shall not be known.

What I tell you in darkness, that speak ye in light: and what ye hear in the ear, that preach ye upon the housetops.

27

And fear not them which kill the body, but are not able to kill the soul: but rather fear him which is able to destroy both soul and body in hell.

28

Are not two sparrows sold for a farthing? and one of them shall not fall on the ground without your Father.

29

But the very hairs of your head are all numbered.                                            30

Fear ye not therefore, ye are of more value than many sparrows.                              31

Whosoever therefore shall confess me before men, him will I confess also before my Father which is in heaven.        32

But whosoever shall deny me before men, him will I also deny before my Father which is in heaven.                   33

For there is nothing covered, that shall not be revealed; neither hid, that shall not be known.        Lk 12: 2

Therefore whatsoever ye have spoken in darkness shall be heard in the light; and that which ye have spoken in the ear in closets shall be proclaimed upon the housetops.                          3

And I say unto you my friends, Be not afraid of them that kill the body, and after that have no more that they can do.        4

But I will forewarn you whom ye shall fear: Fear him, which after he hath killed hath power to cast into hell; yea, I say unto you, Fear him.                          5

Are not five sparrows sold for two farthings, and not one of them is forgotten before God?                          6

But even the very hairs of your head are all numbered. Fear not therefore: ye are of more value than many sparrows.        7

Also I say unto you, Whosoever shall confess me before men, him shall the Son of
man also confess before the angels of God:

8

But he that denieth me before men shall
be denied before the angels of God.

9

Faith will bring divi-
sion in households.

Think not that I am come to send peace
on earth: I came not to send peace, but a
sword.

Mt 10:34

For I am come to set a man at variance
against his father, and the daughter against
her mother, and the daughter in law
against her mother in law.

35

And a man's foes shall be they of his own
household.

36

I am come to send fire on the earth; and
what will I, if it be already kindled?

Lk 12:49

But I have a baptism to be baptized with;
and how am I straitened till it be accomplished!

50

Suppose ye that I am come to give peace
on earth? I tell you, Nay; but rather divi-
sion:

51

For from henceforth there shall be five in
one house divided, three against two, and
two against three.

52

The father shall be divided against the son,
and the son against the father; the mother

53

against the daughter, and the daughter against the mother; the mother in law against her daughter in law, and the daughter in law against her mother in law.

Though the costs of faith be great, its rewards are greater still.

He that loveth father or mother more than me is not worthy of me: and he that loveth son or daughter more than me is not worthy of me.

Mt 10:37

And he that taketh not his cross, and followeth after me, is not worthy of me.

38

He that findeth his life shall lose it: and he that loseth his life for my sake shall find it.

39

He that receiveth you receiveth me, and he that receiveth me receiveth him that sent me.

40

He that receiveth a prophet in the name of a prophet shall receive a prophet's reward; and he that receiveth a righteous man in the name of a righteous man shall receive a righteous man's reward.

41

And whosoever shall give to drink unto one of these little ones a cup of cold water only in the name of a disciple, verily I say unto you, he shall in no wise lose his reward.

42

*Related Saying*

If any man come to me, and hate not his father, and mother, and wife, and children, and brethren, and sisters, yea, and his own life also, he cannot be my disciple.

Lk 14:26

And whosoever doth not bear his cross, and come after me, cannot be my disciple.

27

For which of you, intending to build a tower, sitteth not down first, and counteth the cost, whether he have sufficient to finish it?

28

Lest haply, after he hath laid the foundation, and is not able to finish it, all that behold it begin to mock him,

29

Saying, This man began to build, and was not able to finish.

30

Or what king, going to make war against another king, sitteth not down first, and consulteth whether he be able with ten thousand to meet him that cometh against him with twenty thousand?

31

Or else, while the other is yet a great way off, he sendeth an ambassage, and desireth conditions of peace.

32

So likewise, whosoever he be of you that forsaketh not all that he hath, he cannot be my disciple.

33

Salt is good: but if the salt have lost his savour, wherewith shall it be seasoned?

34

It is neither fit for the land, nor yet for the dunghill; but men cast it out. He that hath ears to hear, let him hear.

35

Jesus responds to
messengers from
John the Baptist,
who ask whether
Jesus be the Christ.

Go and shew John again those things
which ye do hear and see:

Mt 11: 4

The blind receive their sight, and the lame
walk, the lepers are cleansed, and the deaf
hear, the dead are raised up, and the poor
have the gospel preached to them.

5

And blessed is he, whosoever shall not be
offended in me.

6

Go your way, and tell John what things
ye have seen and heard; how that the blind
see, the lame walk, the lepers are cleansed,
the deaf hear, the dead are raised, to the
poor the gospel is preached.

Lk   7:22

And blessed is he, whosoever shall not be
offended in me.

23

He upbraids the
multitude for failing
to recognize John
the Baptist as Elijah
("Elias").

What went ye out into the wilderness to
see? A reed shaken with the wind?

Mt 11: 7

But what went ye out for to see? A man
clothed in soft raiment? behold, they that
wear soft clothing are in kings' houses.

8

But what went ye out for to see? A
prophet? yea, I say unto you, and more
than a prophet.

9

For this is he, of whom it is written, Behold, I send my messenger before thy face, which shall prepare thy way before thee.

10

Verily I say unto you, Among them that are born of women there hath not risen a greater than John the Baptist: notwithstanding he that is least in the kingdom of heaven is greater than he.

11

And from the days of John the Baptist until now the kingdom of heaven suffereth violence, and the violent take it by force.

12

For all the prophets and the law prophesied until John.

13

### Related Saying

The law and the prophets were until John: since that time the kingdom of God is preached, and every man presseth into it.

Lk 16:16

Mt 11 [continued]

And if ye will receive it, this is Elias, which was for to come.

14

He that hath ears to hear, let him hear.

15

But whereunto shall I liken this generation? It is like unto children sitting in the markets, and calling unto their fellows,

16

And saying, We have piped unto you, and ye have not danced; we have mourned unto you, and ye have not lamented.

17

For John came neither eating nor drinking, and they say, He hath a devil.

18

The Son of man came eating and drink- 19
ing, and they say, Behold a man gluttonous, and a winebibber, a friend of
publicans and sinners. But wisdom is justified of her children.

What went ye out into the wilderness for Lk 7:24
to see? A reed shaken with the wind?

But what went ye out for to see? A man 25
clothed in soft raiment? Behold, they
which are gorgeously apparelled, and live
delicately, are in kings' courts.

But what went ye out for to see? A 26
prophet? Yea, I say unto you, and much
more than a prophet.

This is he, of whom it is written, Behold, 27
I send my messenger before thy face,
which shall prepare thy way before thee.

For I say unto you, Among those that are 28
born of women there is not a greater
prophet than John the Baptist: but he that
is least in the kingdom of God is greater
than he.

Whereunto then shall I liken the men of 31
this generation? and to what are they like?

They are like unto children sitting in the 32
marketplace, and calling one to another,
and saying, We have piped unto you, and
ye have not danced; we have mourned to
you, and ye have not wept.

For John the Baptist came neither eating 33
bread nor drinking wine; and ye say, He
hath a devil.

The Son of man is come eating and drinking; and ye say, Behold a gluttonous man, and a winebibber, a friend of publicans and sinners!

34

But wisdom is justified of all her children.

35

He prophesies the judgment of the cities of Galilee.

Woe unto thee, Chorazin! woe unto thee, Bethsaida! for if the mighty works, which were done in you, had been done in Tyre and Sidon, they would have repented long ago in sackcloth and ashes.

Mt 11:21

But I say unto you, It shall be more tolerable for Tyre and Sidon at the day of judgment, than for you.

22

And thou, Capernaum, which art exalted unto heaven, shalt be brought down to hell: for if the mighty works, which have been done in thee, had been done in Sodom, it would have remained until this day.

23

But I say unto you, That it shall be more tolerable for the land of Sodom in the day of judgment, than for thee.

24

Woe unto thee, Chorazin! woe unto thee, Bethsaida! for if the mighty works had been done in Tyre and Sidon, which have been done in you, they had a great while ago repented, sitting in sackcloth and ashes.

Lk 10:13

But it shall be more tolerable for Tyre and
Sidon at the judgment, than for you.

14

And thou, Capernaum, which art exalted
to heaven, shalt be thrust down to hell.

15

He that heareth you heareth me; and he
that despiseth you despiseth me; and he
that despiseth me despiseth him that sent
me.

16

He gives his Father
thanks for wisdom.

I thank thee, O Father, Lord of heaven
and earth, because thou hast hid these
things from the wise and prudent, and
hast revealed them unto babes.

Mt 11:25

Even so, Father: for so it seemed good in
thy sight.

26

All things are delivered unto me of my
Father: and no man knoweth the Son, but
the Father; neither knoweth any man the
Father, save the Son, and he to whomsoever the Son will reveal him.

27

*Related Saying*

I thank thee, O Father, Lord of heaven
and earth, that thou hast hid these things
from the wise and prudent, and hast revealed them unto babes: even so, Father;
for so it seemed good in thy sight.

Lk 10:21

All things are delivered to me of my Father: and no man knoweth who the Son
is, but the Father; and who the Father is,
but the Son, and he to whom the Son will
reveal him.

22

He offers comfort to
the heavy-laden.

Come unto me, all ye that labour and are
heavy laden, and I will give you rest.

Mt 11:28

Take my yoke upon you, and learn of me;
for I am meek and lowly in heart: and ye
shall find rest unto your souls.

29

For my yoke is easy, and my burden is
light.

30

Jesus counters the
Pharisees' charge
that his power
comes from the
Devil.

Every kingdom divided against itself is
brought to desolation; and every city or
house divided against itself shall not stand:

Mt 12:25

And if Satan cast out Satan, he is divided
against himself; how shall then his kingdom stand?

26

And if I by Beelzebub cast out devils, by
whom do your children cast them out?
therefore they shall be your judges.

27

But if I cast out devils by the Spirit of
God, then the kingdom of God is come
unto you.

28

Or else how can one enter into a strong
man's house, and spoil his goods, except
he first bind the strong man? and then he
will spoil his house.

29

He that is not with me is against me; and
he that gathereth not with me scattereth
abroad.

30

Wherefore I say unto you, All manner of sin and blasphemy shall be forgiven unto men: but the blasphemy against the Holy Ghost shall not be forgiven unto men.

31

And whosoever speaketh a word against the Son of man, it shall be forgiven him: but whosoever speaketh against the Holy Ghost, it shall not be forgiven him, neither in this world, neither in the world to come.

32

### Related Saying

And whosoever shall speak a word against the Son of man, it shall be forgiven him: but unto him that blasphemeth against the Holy Ghost it shall not be forgiven.

Lk 12:10

Mt 12 [continued]

Either make the tree good, and his fruit good; or else make the tree corrupt, and his fruit corrupt: for the tree is known by his fruit.

33

O generation of vipers, how can ye, being evil, speak good things? for out of the abundance of the heart the mouth speaketh.

34

A good man out of the good treasure of the heart bringeth forth good things: and an evil man out of the evil treasure bringeth forth evil things.

35

But I say unto you, That every idle word that men shall speak, they shall give account thereof in the day of judgment.

36

For by thy words thou shalt be justified, and by thy words thou shalt be condemned.

37

How can Satan cast out Satan?

Mk 3:23

And if a kingdom be divided against itself, that kingdom cannot stand.

24

And if a house be divided against itself, that house cannot stand.

25

And if Satan rise up against himself, and be divided, he cannot stand, but hath an end.

26

No man can enter into a strong man's house, and spoil his goods, except he will first bind the strong man; and then he will spoil his house.

27

Verily I say unto you, All sins shall be forgiven unto the sons of men, and blasphemies wherewith soever they shall blaspheme:

28

But he that shall blaspheme against the Holy Ghost hath never forgiveness, but is in danger of eternal damnation:

29

Every kingdom divided against itself is brought to desolation; and a house divided against a house falleth.

Lk 11:17

If Satan also be divided against himself, how shall his kingdom stand? because ye say that I cast out devils through Beelzebub.

18

And if I by Beelzebub cast out devils, by whom do your sons cast them out? therefore shall they be your judges.

19

But if I with the finger of God cast out devils, no doubt the kingdom of God is come upon you.

20

When a strong man armed keepeth his palace, his goods are in peace:

21

But when a stronger than he shall come upon him, and overcome him, he taketh from him all his armour wherein he trusted, and divideth his spoils.

22

He that is not with me is against me: and he that gathereth not with me scattereth.

23

He refuses to give them a sign that his power comes from God.

Mt 12:39

An evil and adulterous generation seeketh after a sign; and there shall no sign be given to it, but the sign of the prophet Jonas:

For as Jonas was three days and three nights in the whale's belly; so shall the Son of man be three days and three nights in the heart of the earth.

40

The men of Nineveh shall rise in judgment with this generation, and shall condemn it: because they repented at the preaching of Jonas; and, behold, a greater than Jonas is here.

41

The queen of the south shall rise up in the judgment with this generation, and

42

shall condemn it: for she came from the uttermost parts of the earth to hear the wisdom of Solomon; and, behold, a greater than Solomon is here.

This is an evil generation: they seek a sign; and there shall no sign be given it, but the sign of Jonas the prophet.

Lk 11:29

For as Jonas was a sign unto the Ninevites, so shall also the Son of man be to this generation.

30

The queen of the south shall rise up in the judgment with the men of this gen-eration, and condemn them: for she came from the utmost parts of the earth to hear the wisdom of Solomon; and, behold, a greater than Solomon is here.

31

The men of Nineve shall rise up in the judgment with this generation, and shall condemn it: for they repented at the preaching of Jonas; and, behold, a greater than Jonas is here.

32

To this generation the unclean spirit, when cast out, will return.

When the unclean spirit is gone out of a man, he walketh through dry places, seek-ing rest, and findeth none.

Mt 12:43

Then he saith, I will return into my house from whence I came out; and when he is come, he findeth it empty, swept, and garnished.

44

Then goeth he, and taketh with himself
seven other spirits more wicked than himself, and they enter in and dwell there: and
the last state of that man is worse than
the first. Even so shall it be also unto this
wicked generation.

45

When the unclean spirit is gone out of a
man, he walketh through dry places, seeking rest; and finding none, he saith, I will
return unto my house whence I came out.

Lk 11:24

And when he cometh, he findeth it swept
and garnished.

25

Then goeth he, and taketh to him seven
other spirits more wicked than himself;
and they enter in, and dwell there: and
the last state of that man is worse than
the first.

26

[*Turning to a woman in the multitude who
calls his mother blessed:*]
Yea rather, blessed are they that hear the
word of God, and keep it.

28

Jesus responds to
his mother and his
brethren in the mul-
titude.

Who is my mother? and who are my
brethren?

Mt 12:48

Behold my mother and my brethren!

49

For whosoever shall do the will of my Father which is in heaven, the same is my
brother, and sister, and mother.

50

Who is my mother, or my brethren?     Mk 3:33

Behold my mother and my brethren!     34

For whosoever shall do the will of God,     35
the same is my brother, and my sister, and
mother.

My mother and my brethren are these     Lk 8:21
which hear the word of God, and do it.

**Jesus preaches the kingdom of God in parables:**

*The parable of the sower, with Jesus' reason for speaking in parables and the interpretation of the parable itself*

Behold, a sower went forth to sow;     Mt 13: 3

And when he sowed, some seeds fell by     4
the way side, and the fowls came and devoured them up:

Some fell upon stony places, where they     5
had not much earth: and forthwith they
sprung up, because they had no deepness
of earth:

And when the sun was up, they were     6
scorched; and because they had no root,
they withered away.

And some fell among thorns; and the     7
thorns sprung up, and choked them:

But other fell into good ground, and     8
brought forth fruit, some an hundredfold,
some sixtyfold, some thirtyfold.

Who hath ears to hear, let him hear. 9

Because it is given unto you to know the 11
mysteries of the kingdom of heaven, but
to them it is not given.

For whosoever hath, to him shall be given, 12
and he shall have more abundance: but
whosoever hath not, from him shall be
taken away even that he hath.

Therefore speak I to them in parables: 13
because they seeing see not; and hearing
they hear not, neither do they understand.

And in them is fulfilled the prophecy of 14
Esaias, which saith, By hearing ye shall
hear, and shall not understand; and seeing ye shall see, and shall not perceive:

For this people's heart is waxed gross, and 15
their ears are dull of hearing, and their
eyes they have closed; lest at any time they
should see with their eyes, and hear with
their ears, and should understand with
their heart, and should be converted, and
I should heal them.

But blessed are your eyes, for they see: and 16
your ears, for they hear.

For verily I say unto you, That many 17
prophets and righteous men have desired
to see those things which ye see, and have
not seen them; and to hear those things
which ye hear, and have not heard them.

*Related Saying*
Blessed are the eyes which see the things Lk 10:23
that ye see:

For I tell you, that many prophets and kings have desired to see those things which ye see, and have not seen them; and to hear those things which ye hear, and have not heard them.

24

Mt 13 [continued]

Hear ye therefore the parable of the sower.

18

When any one heareth the word of the kingdom, and understandeth it not, then cometh the wicked one, and catcheth away that which was sown in his heart. This is he which received seed by the way side.

19

But he that received the seed into stony places, the same is he that heareth the word, and anon with joy receiveth it;

20

Yet hath he not root in himself, but dureth for a while: for when tribulation or persecution ariseth because of the word, by and by he is offended.

21

He also that received seed among the thorns is he that heareth the word; and the care of this world, and the deceitfulness of riches, choke the word, and he becometh unfruitful.

22

But he that received seed into the good ground is he that heareth the word, and understandeth it; which also beareth fruit, and bringeth forth, some an hundredfold, some sixty, some thirty.

23

Hearken; Behold, there went out a sower to sow:

Mk 4: 3

And it came to pass, as he sowed, some fell by the way side, and the fowls of the air came and devoured it up.

4

And some fell on stony ground, where it had not much earth; and immediately it sprang up, because it had no depth of earth:

5

But when the sun was up, it was scorched; and because it had no root, it withered away.

6

And some fell among thorns, and the thorns grew up, and choked it, and it yielded no fruit.

7

And other fell on good ground, and did yield fruit that sprang up and increased; and brought forth, some thirty, and some sixty, and some an hundred.

8

He that hath ears to hear, let him hear.

9

Unto you it is given to know the mystery of the kingdom of God: but unto them that are without, all these things are done in parables:

11

That seeing they may see, and not perceive; and hearing they may hear, and not understand; lest at any time they should be converted, and their sins should be forgiven them.

12

Know ye not this parable? and how then will ye know all parables?

13

The sower soweth the word.

14

And these are they by the way side, where the word is sown; but when they have heard, Satan cometh immediately, and taketh away the word that was sown in their hearts. 15

And these are they likewise which are sown on stony ground; who, when they have heard the word, immediately receive it with gladness; 16

And have no root in themselves, and so endure but for a time: afterward, when affliction or persecution ariseth for the word's sake, immediately they are offended. 17

And these are they which are sown among thorns; such as hear the word, 18

And the cares of this world, and the deceitfulness of riches, and the lusts of other things entering in, choke the word, and it becometh unfruitful. 19

And these are they which are sown on good ground; such as hear the word, and receive it, and bring forth fruit, some thirtyfold, some sixty, and some an hundred. 20

Is a candle brought to be put under a bushel, or under a bed? and not to be set on a candlestick? 21

For there is nothing hid, which shall not be manifested; neither was any thing kept secret, but that it should come abroad. 22

If any man have ears to hear, let him hear. 23

Take heed what ye hear: with what mea-    24
sure ye mete, it shall be measured to you:
and unto you that hear shall more be
given.

For he that hath, to him shall be given:    25
and he that hath not, from him shall be
taken even that which he hath.

So is the kingdom of God, as if a man    26
should cast seed into the ground;

And should sleep, and rise night and day,    27
and the seed should spring and grow up,
he knoweth not how.

For the earth bringeth forth fruit of her-    28
self; first the blade, then the ear, after that
the full corn in the ear.

But when the fruit is brought forth, im-    29
mediately he putteth in the sickle, because
the harvest is come.


A sower went out to sow his seed: and as    Lk  8:  5
he sowed, some fell by the way side; and
it was trodden down, and the fowls of the
air devoured it.

And some fell upon a rock; and as soon    6
as it was sprung up, it withered away, because it lacked moisture.

And some fell among thorns; and the    7
thorns sprang up with it, and choked it.

And other fell on good ground, and    8
sprang up, and bare fruit an hundredfold.
He that hath ears to hear, let him hear.

Unto you it is given to know the mysteries of the kingdom of God: but to others in parables; that seeing they might not see, and hearing they might not understand.

10

Now the parable is this: The seed is the word of God.

11

Those by the way side are they that hear; then cometh the devil, and taketh away the word out of their hearts, lest they should believe and be saved.

12

They on the rock are they, which, when they hear, receive the word with joy; and these have no root, which for a while believe, and in time of temptation fall away.

13

And that which fell among thorns are they, which, when they have heard, go forth, and are choked with cares and riches and pleasures of this life, and bring no fruit to perfection.

14

But that on the good ground are they, which in an honest and good heart, having heard the word, keep it, and bring forth fruit with patience.

15

No man, when he hath lighted a candle, covereth it with a vessel, or putteth it under a bed; but setteth it on a candlestick, that they which enter in may see the light.

16

For nothing is secret, that shall not be made manifest; neither any thing hid, that shall not be known and come abroad.

17

Take heed therefore how ye hear: for whosoever hath, to him shall be given; and whosoever hath not, from him shall be taken even that which he seemeth to have.

18

The kingdom of heaven is likened unto a man which sowed good seed in his field:

Mt 13:24

But while men slept, his enemy came and sowed tares among the wheat, and went his way.

25

But when the blade was sprung up, and brought forth fruit, then appeared the tares also.

26

So the servants of the householder came and said unto him, Sir, didst not thou sow good seed in thy field? from whence then hath it tares?

27

He said unto them, An enemy hath done this. The servants said unto him, Wilt thou then that we go and gather them up?

28

But he said, Nay; lest while ye gather up the tares, ye root up also the wheat with them.

29

Let both grow together until the harvest: and in the time of harvest I will say to the reapers, Gather ye together first the tares, and bind them in bundles to burn them: but gather the wheat into my barn.

30

He that soweth the good seed is the Son of man;

37

The field is the world; the good seed are the children of the kingdom; but the tares are the children of the wicked one;

38

The enemy that sowed them is the devil; the harvest is the end of the world; and the reapers are the angels.

39

As therefore the tares are gathered and burned in the fire; so shall it be in the end of this world.

40

The Son of man shall send forth his angels, and they shall gather out of his kingdom all things that offend, and them which do iniquity;

41

And shall cast them into a furnace of fire: there shall be wailing and gnashing of teeth.

42

Then shall the righteous shine forth as the sun in the kingdom of their Father. Who hath ears to hear, let him hear.

43

*The parable of the mustard seed*

The kingdom of heaven is like to a grain of mustard seed, which a man took, and sowed in his field:

Mt 13:31

Which indeed is the least of all seeds: but when it is grown, it is the greatest among herbs, and becometh a tree, so that the birds of the air come and lodge in the branches thereof.

32

Whereunto shall we liken the kingdom of God? or with what comparison shall we compare it?

Mk 4:30

It is like a grain of mustard seed, which, when it is sown in the earth, is less than all the seeds that be in the earth:

31

But when it is sown, it groweth up, and becometh greater than all herbs, and shooteth out great branches; so that the

32

fowls of the air may lodge under the shadow of it.

Unto what is the kingdom of God like? and whereunto shall I resemble it?

Lk 13:18

It is like a grain of mustard seed, which a man took, and cast into his garden; and it grew, and waxed a great tree; and the fowls of the air lodged in the branches of it.

19

*The parable of the leaven*

The kingdom of heaven is like unto leaven, which a woman took, and hid in three measures of meal, till the whole was leavened.

Mt 13:33

Whereunto shall I liken the kingdom of God?

Lk 13:20

It is like leaven, which a woman took and hid in three measures of meal, till the whole was leavened.

21

*Other parables*

Again, the kingdom of heaven is like unto treasure hid in a field; the which when a man hath found, he hideth, and for joy thereof goeth and selleth all that he hath, and buyeth that field.

Mt 13:44

Again, the kingdom of heaven is like unto a merchant man, seeking goodly pearls:

45

Who, when he had found one pearl of great price, went and sold all that he had, and bought it.

46

Again, the kingdom of heaven is like unto a net, that was cast into the sea, and gathered of every kind:

47

Which, when it was full, they drew to shore, and sat down, and gathered the good into vessels, but cast the bad away.

48

So shall it be at the end of the world: the angels shall come forth, and sever the wicked from among the just,

49

And shall cast them into the furnace of fire: there shall be wailing and gnashing of teeth.

50

Have ye understood all these things?

51

Therefore every scribe which is instructed unto the kingdom of heaven is like unto a man that is an householder, which bringeth forth out of his treasure things new and old.

52

Jesus stills a tempest on the Sea of Galilee.

Why are ye fearful, O ye of little faith?

Mt 8:26

Let us pass over unto the other side.

Mk 4:35

Peace, be still.

39

Why are ye so fearful? how is it that ye have no faith?

40

Let us go over unto the other side of the lake.

Lk  8:22

Where is your faith?

25

On the other side of the sea Jesus casts an unclean spirit called "Legion" out of a man and into a herd of swine.

Go.

Mt  8:32

Come out of the man, thou unclean spirit.

Mk  5:  8

What is thy name?

9

Go home to thy friends, and tell them how great things the Lord hath done for thee, and hath had compassion on thee.

19

What is thy name?

Lk  8:30

Return to thine own house, and shew how great things God hath done unto thee.

39

Jesus heals a woman with a hemorrhage and raises the daughter of Jairus, a synagogue official.

Daughter, be of good comfort; thy faith hath made thee whole.

Mt  9:22

Give place: for the maid is not dead, but sleepeth.

24

Who touched my clothes?

Mk  5:30

| | |
|---|---|
| Daughter, thy faith hath made thee whole; go in peace, and be whole of thy plague. | 34 |
| Be not afraid, only believe. | 36 |
| Why make ye this ado, and weep? the damsel is not dead, but sleepeth. | 39 |
| Talitha cumi; *which is, being interpreted, Damsel, I say unto thee, arise.* | 41 |

| | |
|---|---|
| Who touched me? | Lk 8:45 |
| Somebody hath touched me: for I perceive that virtue is gone out of me. | 46 |
| Daughter, be of good comfort: thy faith had made thee whole; go in peace. | 48 |
| Fear not: believe only, and she shall be made whole. | 50 |
| Weep not; she is not dead, but sleepeth. | 52 |
| Maid, arise. | 54 |

He also heals two blind men who have pursued him.

| | |
|---|---|
| Believe ye that I am able to do this? | Mt 9:28 |
| According to your faith be it unto you. | 29 |
| See that no man know it. | 30 |

Jesus can do few mighty works in his own country.

| | |
|---|---|
| A prophet is not without honour, save in his own country, and in his own house. | Mt 13:57 |

A prophet is not without honour, but in his own country, and among his own kin, and in his own house.

Mk 6: 4

The Spirit of the Lord is upon me, because he hath anointed me to preach the gospel to the poor; he hath sent me to heal the brokenhearted, to preach deliverance to the captives, and recovering of sight to the blind, to set at liberty them that are bruised,

Lk 4:18

To preach the acceptable year of the Lord.

19

This day is this scripture fulfilled in your ears.

21

Ye will surely say unto me this proverb, Physician, heal thyself: whatsoever we have heard done in Capernaum, do also here in thy country.

23

Verily I say unto you, No prophet is accepted in his own country.

24

But I tell you of a truth, many widows were in Israel in the days of Elias, when the heaven was shut up three years and six months, when great famine was throughout all the land;

25

But unto none of them was Elias sent, save unto Sarepta, a city of Sidon, unto a woman that was a widow.

26

And many lepers were in Israel in the time of Eliseus the prophet; and none of them was cleansed, saving Naaman the Syrian.

27

Jesus feeds five
thousand followers
with five loaves by
the Sea of Galilee.

| | |
|---|---|
| They need not depart; give ye them to eat. | Mt 14:16 |
| Bring them hither to me. | 18 |
| | |
| Come ye yourselves apart into a desert place, and rest a while: | Mk 6:31 |
| Give ye them to eat. | 37 |
| How many loaves have ye? go and see. | 38 |
| | |
| Give ye them to eat. | Lk 9:13 |
| Make them sit down by fifties in a company. | 14 |
| | |
| Whence shall we buy bread, that these may eat? | Jn 6: 5 |
| Make the men sit down. | 10 |
| Gather up the fragments that remain, that nothing be lost. | 12 |

He comes, walking
on the water, to his
disciples in a ship.

| | |
|---|---|
| Be of good cheer; it is I; be not afraid. | Mt 14:27 |
| Come. | 29 |
| O thou of little faith, wherefore didst thou doubt? | 31 |
| | |
| Be of good cheer: it is I; be not afraid. | Mk 6:50 |

It is I; be not afraid.

Jn 6:20

On reaching
Capernaum he
teaches the multi-
tude that he is the
bread of life.

Verily, verily, I say unto you, Ye seek me, not because ye saw the miracles, but because ye did eat of the loaves, and were filled.

Jn 6:26

Labour not for the meat which perisheth, but for that meat which endureth unto everlasting life, which the Son of man shall give unto you: for him hath God the Father sealed.

27

This is the work of God, that ye believe on him whom he hath sent.

29

Verily, verily, I say unto you, Moses gave you not that bread from heaven; but my Father giveth you the true bread from heaven.

32

For the bread of God is he which cometh down from heaven, and giveth life unto the world.

33

I am the bread of life: he that cometh to me shall never hunger; and he that believeth on me shall never thirst.

35

But I said unto you, That ye also have seen me, and believe not.

36

All that the Father giveth me shall come to me; and him that cometh to me I will in no wise cast out.

37

For I came down from heaven, not to do mine own will, but the will of him that sent me.

38

And this is the Father's will which hath sent me, that of all which he hath given me I should lose nothing, but should raise it up again at the last day.

39

And this is the will of him that sent me, that every one which seeth the Son, and believeth on him, may have everlasting life: and I will raise him up at the last day.

40

Murmur not among yourselves.

43

No man can come to me, except the Father which hath sent me draw him: and I will raise him up at the last day.

44

It is written in the prophets, And they shall be all taught of God. Every man therefore that hath heard, and hath learned of the Father, cometh unto me.

45

Not that any man hath seen the Father, save he which is of God, he hath seen the Father.

46

Verily, verily, I say unto you, He that believeth on me hath everlasting life.

47

I am that bread of life.

48

Your fathers did eat manna in the wilderness, and are dead.

49

This is the bread which cometh down from heaven, that a man may eat thereof, and not die.

50

I am the living bread which came down
from heaven: if any man eat of this bread,
he shall live for ever: and the bread that I
will give is my flesh, which I will give for
the life of the world.

51

Verily, verily, I say unto you, Except ye
eat the flesh of the Son of man, and drink
his blood, ye have no life in you.

53

Whoso eateth my flesh, and drinketh my
blood, hath eternal life; and I will raise
him up at the last day.

54

For my flesh is meat indeed, and my blood
is drink indeed.

55

He that eateth my flesh, and drinketh my
blood, dwelleth in me, and I in him.

56

As the living Father hath sent me, and I
live by the Father: so he that eateth me,
even he shall live by me.

57

This is that bread which came down from
heaven: not as your fathers did eat manna,
and are dead: he that eateth of this bread
shall live for ever.

58

He reproves his dis-
ciples, many of
whom reject this
teaching.

Doth this offend you?

Jn 6:61

What and if ye shall see the Son of man
ascend up where he was before?

62

It is the spirit that quickeneth; the flesh
profiteth nothing: the words that I speak
unto you, they are spirit, and they are life.

63

But there are some of you that believe not. 64

Therefore said I unto you, that no man 65
can come unto me, except it were given
unto him of my Father.

Will ye also go away? 67

Have not I chosen you twelve, and one of 70
you is a devil?

Pharisees from
Jerusalem invoke
the purity laws
against Jesus, who
denounces their hy-
pocrisy.

Why do ye also transgress the command- Mt 15: 3
ment of God by your tradition?

For God commanded, saying, Honour 4
thy father and mother: and, He that
curseth father or mother, let him die the
death.

But ye say, Whosoever shall say to his fa- 5
ther or his mother, It is a gift, by whatsoever thou mightest be profited by me;

And honour not his father or his mother, 6
he shall be free. Thus have ye made the
commandment of God of none effect by
your tradition.

Ye hypocrites, well did Esaias prophesy of 7
you, saying,

This people draweth nigh unto me with 8
their mouth, and honoureth me with their
lips; but their heart is far from me.

But in vain they do worship me, teaching 9
for doctrines the commandments of men.

Hear, and understand:                              10

Not that which goeth into the mouth          11
defileth a man; but that which cometh
out of the mouth, this defileth a man.

Every plant, which my heavenly Father      13
hath not planted, shall be rooted up.

Let them alone: they be blind leaders of    14
the blind. And if the blind lead the blind,
both shall fall into the ditch.

Are ye also yet without understanding?      16

Do not ye yet understand, that whatso-      17
ever entereth in at the mouth goeth into
the belly, and is cast out into the draught?

But those things which proceed out of the   18
mouth come forth from the heart; and
they defile the man.

For out of the heart proceed evil thoughts, 19
murders, adulteries, fornications, thefts,
false witness, blasphemies:

These are the things which defile a man:     20
but to eat with unwashen hands defileth
not a man.


Well hath Esaias prophesied of you hypo-   Mk 7: 6
crites, as it is written, This people
honoureth me with their lips, but their
heart is far from me.

Howbeit in vain do they worship me,          7
teaching for doctrines the commandments of men.

For laying aside the commandment of        8
God, ye hold the tradition of men, as the

washing of pots and cups: and many other such like things ye do.

Full well ye reject the commandment of God, that ye may keep your own tradition.    9

For Moses said, Honour thy father and thy mother; and, Whoso curseth father or mother, let him die the death:    10

But ye say, If a man shall say to his father or mother, It is Corban, that is to say, a gift, by whatsoever thou mightest be profited by me; he shall be free.    11

And ye suffer him no more to do ought for his father or his mother;    12

Making the word of God of none effect through your tradition, which ye have delivered: and many such like things do ye.    13

Hearken unto me every one of you, and understand:    14

There is nothing from without a man, that entering into him can defile him: but the things which come out of him, those are they that defile the man.    15

If any man have ears to hear, let him hear.    16

Are ye so without understanding also? Do ye not perceive, that whatsoever thing from without entereth into the man, it cannot defile him;    18

Because it entereth not into his heart, but into the belly, and goeth out into the draught, purging all meats?    19

That which cometh out of the man, that defileth the man.

20

For from within, out of the heart of men, proceed evil thoughts, adulteries, fornications, murders,

21

Thefts, covetousness, wickedness, deceit, lasciviousness, an evil eye, blasphemy, pride, foolishness:

22

All these evil things come from within, and defile the man.

23

Jesus heals a
Syrophoenician
woman's daughter.

I am not sent but unto the lost sheep of the house of Israel.

Mt 15:24

It is not meet to take the children's bread, and to cast it to dogs.

26

O woman, great is thy faith: be it unto thee even as thou wilt.

28

Let the children first be filled: for it is not meet to take the children's bread, and to cast it unto the dogs.

Mk 7:27

For this saying go thy way; the devil is gone out of thy daughter.

29

He heals a deaf
man.

Ephphatha, *that is, Be opened.*

Mk 7:34

Jesus feeds four thousand followers with seven loaves.

I have compassion on the multitude, because they continue with me now three days, and have nothing to eat: and I will not send them away fasting, lest they faint in the way.

Mt 15:32

How many loaves have ye?

34

I have compassion on the multitude, because they have now been with me three days, and have nothing to eat:

Mk 8: 2

And if I send them away fasting to their own houses, they will faint by the way.

3

How many loaves have ye?

5

Jesus cautions his disciples against the hypocrisy of the Pharisees, who ask him to show them a sign.

When it is evening, ye say, It will be fair weather: for the sky is red.

Mt 16: 2

And in the morning, It will be foul weather to day: for the sky is red and lowring. O ye hypocrites, ye can discern the face of the sky; but can ye not discern the signs of the times?

3

A wicked and adulterous generation seeketh after a sign; and there shall no sign be given unto it, but the sign of the prophet Jonas.

4

Take heed and beware of the leaven of the       6
Pharisees and of the Sadducees.

O ye of little faith, why reason ye among       8
yourselves, because ye have brought no
bread?

Do ye not yet understand, neither remem-       9
ber the five loaves of the five thousand,
and how many baskets ye took up?

Neither the seven loaves of the four thou-       10
sand, and how many baskets ye took up?

How is it that ye do not understand that       11
I spake it not to you concerning bread,
that ye should beware of the leaven of the
Pharisees and of the Sadducees?

Why doth this generation seek after a sign?    Mk 8:12
verily I say unto you, There shall no sign
be given unto this generation.

Take heed, beware of the leaven of the       15
Pharisees, and of the leaven of Herod.

Why reason ye, because ye have no bread?       17
perceive ye not yet, neither understand?
have ye your heart yet hardened?

Having eyes, see ye not? and having ears,       18
hear ye not? and do ye not remember?

When I brake the five loaves among five       19
thousand, how many baskets full of fragments took ye up?

And when the seven among four thou-       20
sand, how many baskets full of fragments
took ye up?

How is it that ye do not understand?                     21

Beware ye of the leaven of the Pharisees,     Lk 12: 1
which is hypocrisy.

When ye see a cloud rise out of the west,                54
straightway ye say, There cometh a shower;
and so it is.

And when ye see the south wind blow, ye                  55
say, There will be heat; and it cometh to
pass.

Ye hypocrites, ye can discern the face of                56
the sky and of the earth; but how is it that
ye do not discern this time?

Jesus heals a blind
man.

Neither go into the town, nor tell it to      Mk 8:26
any in the town.

Jesus blesses Peter
for affirming that he
is the Christ but
also rebukes Peter
for denying he must
suffer, die and rise
again.

Whom do men say that I the Son of man         Mt 16:13
am?

But whom say ye that I am?                               15

Blessed art thou, Simon Bar-jona: for flesh              17
and blood hath not revealed it unto thee,
but my Father which is in heaven.

And I say also unto thee, That thou art                  18
Peter, and upon this rock I will build my

church; and the gates of hell shall not prevail against it.

And I will give unto thee the keys of the     19
kingdom of heaven: and whatsoever thou
shalt bind on earth shall be bound in
heaven: and whatsoever thou shalt loose
on earth shall be loosed in heaven.

Get thee behind me, Satan: thou art an     23
offence unto me: for thou savourest not
the things that be of God, but those that
be of men.

If any man will come after me, let him     24
deny himself, and take up his cross, and
follow me.

For whosoever will save his life shall lose     25
it: and whosoever will lose his life for my
sake shall find it.

For what is a man profited, if he shall gain     26
the whole world, and lose his own soul?
or what shall a man give in exchange for
his soul?

For the Son of man shall come in the glory     27
of his Father with his angels; and then he
shall reward every man according to his
works.

Verily I say unto you, There be some     28
standing here, which shall not taste of
death, till they see the Son of man coming in his kingdom.

Whom do men say that I am?     Mk 8:27

But whom say ye that I am?     29

Get thee behind me, Satan: for thou savourest not the things that be of God, but the things that be of men. 33

Whosoever will come after me, let him deny himself, and take up his cross, and follow me. 34

For whosoever will save his life shall lose it; but whosoever shall lose his life for my sake and the gospel's, the same shall save it. 35

For what shall it profit a man, if he shall gain the whole world, and lose his own soul? 36

Or what shall a man give in exchange for his soul? 37

Whosoever therefore shall be ashamed of me and of my words in this adulterous and sinful generation; of him also shall the Son of man be ashamed, when he cometh in the glory of his Father with the holy angels. 38

Verily I say unto you, That there be some of them that stand here, which shall not taste of death, till they have seen the kingdom of God come with power. Mk 9: 1

Whom say the people that I am? Lk 9:18

But whom say ye that I am? 20

The Son of man must suffer many things, and be rejected of the elders and chief priests and scribes, and be slain, and be raised the third day. 22

If any man will come after me, let him deny himself, and take up his cross daily, and follow me.

23

For whosoever will save his life shall lose it: but whosoever will lose his life for my sake, the same shall save it.

24

For what is a man advantaged, if he gain the whole world, and lose himself, or be cast away?

25

For whosoever shall be ashamed of me and of my words, of him shall the Son of man be ashamed, when he shall come in his own glory, and in his Father's, and of the holy angels.

26

But I tell you of a truth, there be some standing here, which shall not taste of death, till they see the kingdom of God.

27

Jesus is transfigured on a high mountain before the eyes of Peter, James and John.

Arise, and be not afraid.

Mt 17: 7

Tell the vision to no man, until the Son of man be risen again from the dead.

9

Elias truly shall first come, and restore all things.

11

But I say unto you, That Elias is come already, and they knew him not, but have done unto him whatsoever they listed. Likewise shall also the Son of man suffer of them.

12

Elias verily cometh first, and restoreth all things; and how it is written of the Son of man, that he must suffer many things, and be set at nought.

Mk 9:12

But I say unto you, That Elias is indeed come, and they have done unto him whatsoever they listed, as it is written of him.

13

Jesus heals an epileptic his disciples could not heal because of their unbelief.

O faithless and perverse generation, how long shall I be with you? how long shall I suffer you? bring him hither to me.

Mt 17:17

Because of your unbelief: for verily I say unto you, If ye have faith as a grain of mustard seed, ye shall say unto this mountain, Remove hence to yonder place; and it shall remove; and nothing shall be impossible unto you.

20

Howbeit this kind goeth not out but by prayer and fasting.

21

What question ye with them?

Mk 9:16

O faithless generation, how long shall I be with you? how long shall I suffer you? bring him unto me.

19

How long is it ago since this came unto him?

21

If thou canst believe, all things are possible to him that believeth.

23

Thou dumb and deaf spirit, I charge thee, come out of him, and enter no more into him.

25

This kind can come forth by nothing, but by prayer and fasting.

29

O faithless and perverse generation, how long shall I be with you, and suffer you? Bring thy son hither.

Lk  9:41

The disciples forbid a man to heal in Jesus' name but Jesus tells them not to do so.

Forbid him not: for there is no man which shall do a miracle in my name, that can lightly speak evil of me.

Mk  9:39

For he that is not against us is on our part.

40

Forbid him not: for he that is not against us is for us.

Lk  9:50

Jesus once more foresees that he must die and rise again.

The Son of man shall be betrayed into the hands of men:

Mt 17:22

And they shall kill him, and the third day he shall be raised again.

23

The Son of man is delivered into the hands of men, and they shall kill him; and

Mk  9:31

after that he is killed, he shall rise the third day.

Let these sayings sink down into your ears: for the Son of man shall be delivered into the hands of men.

Lk  9:44

Jesus is asked to pay the Temple tax.

What thinkest thou, Simon? of whom do the kings of the earth take custom or tribute? of their own children, or of strangers?

Mt 17:25

Then are the children free.

26

Notwithstanding, lest we should offend them, go thou to the sea, and cast an hook, and take up the fish that first cometh up; and when thou hast opened his mouth, thou shalt find a piece of money: that take, and give unto them for me and thee.

27

The disciples dispute among themselves who shall be greatest.

Verily I say unto you, Except ye be converted, and become as little children, ye shall not enter into the kingdom of heaven.

Mt 18: 3

Whosoever therefore shall humble himself as this little child, the same is greatest in the kingdom of heaven.

4

And whoso shall receive one such little child in my name receiveth me.

5

What was it that ye disputed among yourselves by the way?

Mk 9:33

If any man desire to be first, the same shall
be last of all, and servant of all.

35

Whosoever shall receive one of such children in my name, receiveth me: and whosoever shall receive me, receiveth not me,
but him that sent me.

37

Whosoever shall receive this child in my
name receiveth me: and whosoever shall
receive me receiveth him that sent me: for
he that is least among you all, the same
shall be great.

Lk 9:48

Jesus teaches them
about temptations
to sin ("offences").

But whoso shall offend one of these little
ones which believe in me, it were better
for him that a millstone were hanged
about his neck, and that he were drowned
in the depth of the sea.

Mt 18: 6

Woe unto the world because of offences!
for it must needs be that offences come;
but woe to that man by whom the offence
cometh!

7

Wherefore if thy hand or thy foot offend
thee, cut them off, and cast them from
thee: it is better for thee to enter into life
halt or maimed, rather than having two
hands or two feet to be cast into everlasting fire.

8

And if thine eye offend thee, pluck it out, and cast it from thee: it is better for thee to enter into life with one eye, rather than having two eyes to be cast into hell fire.

9

For whosoever shall give you a cup of water to drink in my name, because ye belong to Christ, verily I say unto you, he shall not lose his reward.

Mk 9:41

And whosoever shall offend one of these little ones that believe in me, it is better for him that a millstone were hanged about his neck, and he were cast into the sea.

42

And if thy hand offend thee, cut it off: it is better for thee to enter into life maimed, than having two hands to go into hell, into the fire that never shall be quenched:

43

Where their worm dieth not, and the fire is not quenched.

44

And if thy foot offend thee, cut it off: it is better for thee to enter halt into life, than having two feet to be cast into hell, into the fire that never shall be quenched:

45

Where their worm dieth not, and the fire is not quenched.

46

And if thine eye offend thee, pluck it out: it is better for thee to enter into the kingdom of God with one eye, than having two eyes to be cast into hell fire:

47

Where their worm dieth not, and the fire is not quenched.

48

For every one shall be salted with fire, and every sacrifice shall be salted with salt.

49

Salt is good: but if the salt have lost his saltness, wherewith will ye season it? Have salt in yourselves, and have peace one with another.

50

It is impossible but that offences will come: but woe unto him, through whom they come!

Lk 17: 1

It were better for him that a millstone were hanged about his neck, and he cast into the sea, than that he should offend one of these little ones.

2

He tells them the parable of the lost sheep.

Take heed that ye despise not one of these little ones; for I say unto you, That in heaven their angels do always behold the face of my Father which is in heaven.

Mt 18:10

For the Son of man is come to save that which was lost.

11

How think ye? if a man have an hundred sheep, and one of them be gone astray, doth he not leave the ninety and nine, and goeth into the mountains, and seeketh that which is gone astray?

12

And if so be that he find it, verily I say unto you, he rejoiceth more of that sheep, than of the ninety and nine which went not astray.

13

Even so it is not the will of your Father
which is in heaven, that one of these little
ones should perish.

14

*Related Saying*

What man of you, having an hundred
sheep, if he lose one of them, doth not
leave the ninety and nine in the wilderness, and go after that which is lost, until
he find it?

Lk 15: 4

And when he hath found it, he layeth it
on his shoulders, rejoicing.

5

And when he cometh home, he calleth
together his friends and neighbours, saying unto them, Rejoice with me; for I have
found my sheep which was lost.

6

I say unto you, that likewise joy shall be
in heaven over one sinner that repenteth,
more than over ninety and nine just persons, which need no repentance.

7

He teaches about
forgiveness.

Moreover if thy brother shall trespass
against thee, go and tell him his fault between thee and him alone: if he shall hear
thee, thou hast gained thy brother.

Mt 18:15

But if he will not hear thee, then take with
thee one or two more, that in the mouth
of two or three witnesses every word may
be established.

16

And if he shall neglect to hear them, tell
it unto the church: but if he neglect to

17

hear the church, let him be unto thee as an heathen man and a publican.

Verily I say unto you, Whatsoever ye shall bind on earth shall be bound in heaven: and whatsoever ye shall loose on earth shall be loosed in heaven.  18

Again I say unto you, That if two of you shall agree on earth as touching any thing that they shall ask, it shall be done for them of my Father which is in heaven.  19

For where two or three are gathered together in my name, there am I in the midst of them.  20

I say not unto thee, Until seven times: but, Until seventy times seven.  22

Take heed to yourselves: If thy brother trespass against thee, rebuke him; and if he repent, forgive him.  Lk 17: 3

And if he trespass against thee seven times in a day, and seven times in a day turn again to thee, saying, I repent; thou shalt forgive him.  4

He illustrates his teaching with the parable of the unforgiving servant.

Therefore is the kingdom of heaven likened unto a certain king, which would take account of his servants.  Mt 18:23

And when he had begun to reckon, one was brought unto him, which owed him ten thousand talents.  24

But forasmuch as he had not to pay, his
lord commanded him to be sold, and his
wife, and children, and all that he had,
and payment to be made.

25

The servant therefore fell down, and worshipped him, saying, Lord, have patience
with me, and I will pay thee all.

26

Then the lord of that servant was moved
with compassion, and loosed him, and
forgave him the debt.

27

But the same servant went out, and found
one of his fellowservants, which owed him
an hundred pence: and he laid hands on
him, and took him by the throat, saying,
Pay me that thou owest.

28

And his fellowservant fell down at his feet,
and besought him, saying, Have patience
with me, and I will pay thee all.

29

And he would not: but went and cast him
into prison, till he should pay the debt.

30

So when his fellowservants saw what was
done, they were very sorry, and came and
told unto their lord all that was done.

31

Then his lord, after that he had called him,
said unto him, O thou wicked servant, I
forgave thee all that debt, because thou
desiredst me:

32

Shouldest not thou also have had compassion on thy fellowservant, even as I had
pity on thee?

33

And his lord was wroth, and delivered him
to the tormentors, till he should pay all
that was due unto him.

34

So likewise shall my heavenly Father do also unto you, if ye from your hearts forgive not every one his brother their trespasses.

35

Jesus sends his brethren to the Feast of Tabernacles in Jerusalem before setting off alone for it.

My time is not yet come: but your time is alway ready.

Jn 7: 6

The world cannot hate you; but me it hateth, because I testify of it, that the works thereof are evil.

7

Go ye up unto this feast: I go not up yet unto this feast; for my time is not yet full come.

8

Jesus is refused hospitality on the way.

Ye know not what manner of spirit ye are of.

Lk 9:55

For the Son of man is not come to destroy men's lives, but to save them.

56

He responds to the half-heartedness of would-be disciples.

The foxes have holes, and the birds of the air have nests; but the Son of man hath not where to lay his head.

Mt 8:20

Follow me; and let the dead bury their dead.

22

Foxes have holes, and birds of the air have nests; but the Son of man hath not where to lay his head.

Lk 9:58

Follow me.

59

Let the dead bury their dead: but go thou and preach the kingdom of god.

60

No man, having put his hand to the plough, and looking back, is fit for the kingdom of God.

62

Having arrived in Jerusalem, Jesus preaches frequently in the Temple about his work as that of God, his Father.

My doctrine is not mine, but his that sent me.

Jn 7:16

If any man will do his will, he shall know of the doctrine, whether it be of God, or whether I speak of myself.

17

He that speaketh of himself seeketh his own glory: but he that seeketh his glory that sent him, the same is true, and no unrighteousness is in him.

18

Did not Moses give you the law, and yet none of you keepeth the law? Why go ye about to kill me?

19

I have done one work, and ye all marvel.

21

Moses therefore gave unto you circumcision; (not because it is of Moses, but of the fathers;) and ye on the sabbath day circumcise a man.

22

If a man on the sabbath day receive circum- 23
cision, that the law of Moses should not be
broken; are ye angry at me, because I have
made a man every whit whole on the sabbath day?

Judge not according to the appearance, but 24
judge righteous judgment.

Ye both know me, and ye know whence I 28
am: and I am not come of myself, but he
that sent me is true, whom ye know not.

But I know him: for I am from him, and he 29
hath sent me.

Yet a little while am I with you, and then I 33
go unto him that sent me.

Ye shall seek me, and shall not find me: and 34
where I am, thither ye cannot come.

If any man thirst, let him come unto me, 37
and drink.

He that believeth on me, as the scripture 38
hath said, out of his belly shall flow rivers
of living water.

The Pharisees bring to
Jesus in the Temple a
woman they are about
to stone for adultery
but, on hearing Jesus'
words, they merely
walk away. Jesus then
testifies to the Phari-
sees of himself as the
Son of God, where-
upon they undertake
to stone him for blas-
phemy.

He that is without sin among you, let him Jn 8: 7
first cast a stone at her.

Woman, where are those thine accusers? 10
hath no man condemned thee?

Neither do I condemn thee: go, and sin 11
no more.

I am the light of the world: he that 12
followeth me shall not walk in darkness,
but shall have the light of life.

Though I bear record of myself, yet my 14
record is true: for I know whence I came,
and whither I go; but ye cannot tell whence
I come, and whither I go.

Ye judge after the flesh; I judge no man. 15

And yet if I judge, my judgment is true: 16
for I am not alone, but I and the Father
that sent me.

It is also written in your law, that the testi- 17
mony of two men is true.

I am one that bear witness of myself, and 18
the Father that sent me beareth witness of
me.

Ye neither know me, nor my Father: if ye 19
had known me, ye should have known my
Father also.

I go my way, and ye shall seek me, and 21
shall die in your sins: whither I go, ye cannot come.

Ye are from beneath; I am from above: ye 23
are of this world; I am not of this world.

I said therefore unto you, that ye shall die 24
in your sins: for if ye believe not that I am
he, ye shall die in your sins.

Even the same that I said unto you from the beginning.    25

I have many things to say and to judge of you: but he that sent me is true; and I speak to the world those things which I have heard of him.    26

When ye have lifted up the Son of man, then shall ye know that I am he, and that I do nothing of myself; but as my Father hath taught me, I speak these things.    28

And he that sent me is with me: the Father hath not left me alone; for I do always those things that please him.    29

If ye continue in my word, then are ye my disciples indeed;    31

And ye shall know the truth, and the truth shall make you free.    32

Verily, verily, I say unto you, Whosoever committeth sin is the servant of sin.    34

And the servant abideth not in the house for ever: but the Son abideth ever.    35

If the Son therefore shall make you free, ye shall be free indeed.    36

I know that ye are Abraham's seed; but ye seek to kill me, because my word hath no place in you.    37

I speak that which I have seen with my Father: and ye do that which ye have seen with your father.    38

If ye were Abraham's children, ye would do the works of Abraham.    39

But now ye seek to kill me, a man that hath told you the truth, which I have heard of God: this did not Abraham.   40

Ye do the deeds of your father.   41

If God were your Father, ye would love me: for I proceeded forth and came from God; neither came I of myself, but he sent me.   42

Why do ye not understand my speech? even because ye cannot hear my word.   43

Ye are of your father the devil, and the lusts of your father ye will do. He was a murderer from the beginning, and abode not in the truth, because there is no truth in him. When he speaketh a lie, he speaketh of his own: for he is a liar, and the father of it.   44

And because I tell you the truth, ye believe me not.   45

Which of you convinceth me of sin? And if I say the truth, why do ye not believe me?   46

He that is of God heareth God's words: ye therefore hear them not, because ye are not of God.   47

I have not a devil; but I honour my Father, and ye do dishonour me.   49

And I seek not mine own glory: there is one that seeketh and judgeth.   50

Verily, verily, I say unto you, If a man keep my saying, he shall never see death.   51

If I honour myself, my honour is nothing: it is my Father that honoureth me; of whom ye say, that he is your God:    54

Yet ye have not known him; but I know him: and if I should say, I know him not, I shall be a liar like unto you: but I know him, and keep his saying.    55

Your father Abraham rejoiced to see my day: and he saw it, and was glad.    56

Verily, verily, I say unto you, Before Abraham was, I am.    58

A blind man whom Jesus heals on the Sabbath sees that Jesus comes from God whereas the Pharisees who expel the man from their synagogue turn out to be spiritually blind: when Jesus tells them the parable of the good shepherd, they do not see.

Neither hath this man sinned, nor his parents: but that the works of God should be made manifest in him.    Jn 9: 3

I must work the works of him that sent me, while it is day: the night cometh, when no man can work.    4

As long as I am in the world, I am the light of the world.    5

Go, wash in the pool of Siloam, *(which is by interpretation, Sent.)*    7

Dost thou believe on the Son of God?    35

Thou hast both seen him, and it is he that    37
talketh with thee.

For judgment I am come into this world,    39
that they which see not might see; and that
they which see might be made blind.

If ye were blind, ye should have no sin: but    41
now ye say, We see; therefore your sin
remaineth.

Verily, verily, I say unto you, He that entereth    Jn 10: 1
not by the door into the sheepfold, but
climbeth up some other way, the same is a
thief and a robber.

But he that entereth in by the door is the    2
shepherd of the sheep.

To him the porter openeth; and the sheep    3
hear his voice: and he calleth his own sheep
by name, and leadeth them out.

And when he putteth forth his own sheep,    4
he goeth before them, and the sheep follow
him: for they know his voice.

And a stranger will they not follow, but will    5
flee from him: for they know not the voice
of strangers.

Verily, verily, I say unto you, I am the door    7
of the sheep.

All that ever came before me are thieves and    8
robbers: but the sheep did not hear them.

I am the door: by me if any man enter in,    9
he shall be saved, and shall go in and out,
and find pasture.

The thief cometh not, but for to steal, and  10
to kill, and to destroy: I am come that
they might have life, and that they might
have it more abundantly.

I am the good shepherd: the good shep-  11
herd giveth his life for the sheep.

But he that is an hireling, and not the  12
shepherd, whose own the sheep are not,
seeth the wolf coming, and leaveth the
sheep, and fleeth: and the wolf catcheth
them, and scattereth the sheep.

The hireling fleeth, because he is an hire-  13
ling, and careth not for the sheep.

I am the good shepherd, and know my  14
sheep, and am known of mine.

As the Father knoweth me, even so know  15
I the Father: and I lay down my life for
the sheep.

And other sheep I have, which are not of  16
this fold: them also I must bring, and they
shall hear my voice; and there shall be one
fold, and one shepherd.

Therefore doth my Father love me, be-  17
cause I lay down my life, that I might take
it again.

No man taketh it from me, but I lay it  18
down of myself. I have power to lay it
down, and I have power to take it again.
This commandment have I received of my
Father.

In answer to a lawyer's question about how to inherit eternal life, Jesus tells the parable of the good Samaritan.

What is written in the law? how readest thou?

Lk 10:26

Thou hast answered right: this do, and thou shalt live.

28

A certain man went down from Jerusalem to Jericho, and fell among thieves, which stripped him of his raiment, and wounded him, and departed, leaving him half dead.

30

And by chance there came down a certain priest that way: and when he saw him, he passed by on the other side.

31

And likewise a Levite, when he was at the place, came and looked on him, and passed by on the other side.

32

But a certain Samaritan, as he journeyed, came where he was: and when he saw him, he had compassion on him,

33

And went to him, and bound up his wounds, pouring in oil and wine, and set him on his own beast, and brought him to an inn, and took care of him.

34

And on the morrow when he departed, he took out two pence, and gave them to the host, and said unto him, Take care of him; and whatsoever thou spendest more, when I come again, I will repay thee.

35

Which now of these three, thinkest thou, was neighbour unto him that fell among the thieves?

36

Go, and do thou likewise.

37

Jesus evaluates the roles of Mary as disciple and Martha as housekeeper.

Martha, Martha, thou art careful and troubled about many things:

Lk 10:41

But one thing is needful: and Mary hath chosen that good part, which shall not be taken away from her.

42

He denounces the hypocrisy of Pharisees and lawyers.

Now do ye Pharisees make clean the outside of the cup and the platter; but your inward part is full of ravening and wickedness.

Lk 11:39

Ye fools, did not he that made that which is without make that which is within also?

40

But rather give alms of such things as ye have; and, behold, all things are clean unto you.

41

But woe unto you, Pharisees! for ye tithe mint and rue and all manner of herbs, and pass over judgment and the love of God: these ought ye to have done, and not to leave the other undone.

42

Woe unto you, Pharisees! for ye love the uppermost seats in the synagogues, and greetings in the markets. 43

Woe unto you, scribes and Pharisees, hypocrites! for ye are as graves which appear not, and the men that walk over them are not aware of them. 44

Woe unto you also, ye lawyers! for ye lade men with burdens grievous to be borne, and ye yourselves touch not the burdens with one of your fingers. 46

Woe unto you! for ye build the sepulchres of the prophets, and your fathers killed them. 47

Truly ye bear witness that ye allow the deeds of your fathers: for they indeed killed them, and ye build their sepulchres. 48

Therefore also said the wisdom of God, I will send them prophets and apostles, and some of them they shall slay and persecute: 49

That the blood of all the prophets, which was shed from the foundation of the world, may be required of this generation; 50

From the blood of Abel unto the blood of Zacharias, which perished between the altar and the temple: verily I say unto you, It shall be required of this generation. 51

Woe unto you, lawyers! for ye have taken away the key of knowledge: ye entered not in yourselves, and them that were entering in ye hindered. 52

In answer to a would-be heir's request for adjudication, Jesus tells the parable of the rich fool.

Man, who made me a judge or a divider over you?

Lk 12:14

Take heed, and beware of covetousness: for a man's life consisteth not in the abundance of the things which he possesseth.

15

The ground of a certain rich man brought forth plentifully:

16

And he thought within himself, saying, What shall I do, because I have no room where to bestow my fruits?

17

And he said, This will I do: I will pull down my barns, and build greater; and there will I bestow all my fruits and my goods.

18

And I will say to my soul, Soul, thou hast much goods laid up for many years; take thine ease, eat, drink, and be merry.

19

But God said unto him, Thou fool, this night thy soul shall be required of thee: then whose shall those things be, which thou hast provided?

20

So is he that layeth up treasure for himself, and is not rich toward God.

21

He preaches repentance and, by way of illustration, tells the parable of the fig tree.

Suppose ye that these Galilaeans were sinners above all the Galilaeans, because they suffered such things?

Lk 13: 2

I tell you, Nay: but, except ye repent, ye shall all likewise perish.

3

Or those eighteen, upon whom the tower in Siloam fell, and slew them, think ye that they were sinners above all men that dwelt in Jerusalem?

4

I tell you, Nay: but, except ye repent, ye shall all likewise perish.

5

A certain man had a fig tree planted in his vineyard; and he came and sought fruit thereon, and found none.

6

Then said he unto the dresser of his vineyard, Behold, these three years I come seeking fruit on this fig tree, and find none: cut it down; why cumbereth it the ground?

7

And he answering said unto him, Lord, let it alone this year also, till I shall dig about it, and dung it:

8

And if it bear fruit, well: and if not, then after that thou shalt cut it down.

9

Jesus heals a woman on the Sabbath and thereby incurs charges of breaking the Sabbath laws.

Woman, thou art loosed from thine infirmity.

Lk 13:12

Thou hypocrite, doth not each one of you on the sabbath loose his ox or his ass from the stall, and lead him away to watering?

15

And ought not this woman, being a daughter of Abraham, whom Satan hath bound, lo, these eighteen years, be loosed from this bond on the sabbath day?

16

At the Feast of the Dedication Jesus identifies himself in the Temple as the Son of God and, having thus once more risked being stoned for blasphemy, withdraws into the wilderness.

I told you, and ye believed not: the works that I do in my Father's name, they bear witness of me.

Jn 10:25

But ye believe not, because ye are not of my sheep, as I said unto you.

26

My sheep hear my voice, and I know them, and they follow me:

27

And I give unto them eternal life; and they shall never perish, neither shall any man pluck them out of my hand.

28

My Father, which gave them me, is greater than all; and no man is able to pluck them out of my Father's hand.

29

I and my Father are one.

30

Many good works have I shewed you from my Father; for which of those works do ye stone me?

32

Is it not written in your law, I said, Ye are gods?

34

If he called them gods, unto whom the word of God came, and the scripture cannot be broken;     35

Say ye of him, whom the Father hath sanctified, and sent into the world, Thou blasphemest; because I said, I am the Son of God?     36

If I do not the works of my Father, believe me not.     37

But if I do, though ye believe not me, believe the works: that ye may know, and believe, that the Father is in me, and I in him.     38

Scorning the Pharisees' warnings that Herod will kill him, Jesus once more journeys towards Jerusalem.

Go ye, and tell that fox, Behold, I cast out devils, and I do cures to day and to morrow, and the third day I shall be perfected.     Lk 13:32

Nevertheless I must walk to day, and to morrow, and the day following: for it cannot be that a prophet perish out of Jerusalem.     33

Jesus justifies healing a man with edema ("the dropsy") on the Sabbath.*

Is it lawful to heal on the sabbath day?     Lk 14: 3

---

* On this occasion Jesus, who is eating with lawyers and Pharisees, tells the parable of the great supper cited under the parable of the royal marriage feast below.

Which of you shall have an ass or an ox fallen into a pit, and will not straightway pull him out on the sabbath day?

5

In answer to the scribes' and Pharisees' charge that he keeps company with publicans and sinners, Jesus tells parables:*

*The parable of the lost coin*

Either what woman having ten pieces of silver, if she lose one piece, doth not light a candle, and sweep the house, and seek diligently till she find it?

Lk 15: 8

And when she hath found it, she calleth her friends and her neighbours together, saying, Rejoice with me; for I have found the piece which I had lost.

9

Likewise, I say unto you, there is joy in the presence of the angels of God over one sinner that repenteth.

10

*The parable of the prodigal son*

A certain man had two sons:

Lk 15: 11

And the younger of them said to his father, Father, give me the portion of goods that falleth to me. And he divided unto them his living.

12

And not many days after the younger son gathered all together, and took his jour-

13

---

* On this occasion Jesus also tells the parable of the lost sheep cited under Mt 18 above.

ney into a far country, and there wasted his substance with riotous living.

And when he had spent all, there arose a mighty famine in that land; and he began to be in want.     14

And he went and joined himself to a citizen of that country; and he sent him into his fields to feed swine.     15

And he would fain have filled his belly with the husks that the swine did eat: and no man gave unto him.     16

And when he came to himself, he said, How many hired servants of my father's have bread enough and to spare, and I perish with hunger!     17

I will arise and go to my father, and will say unto him, Father, I have sinned against heaven, and before thee,     18

And am no more worthy to be called thy son: make me as one of thy hired servants.     19

And he arose, and came to his father. But when he was yet a great way off, his father saw him, and had compassion, and ran, and fell on his neck, and kissed him.     20

And the son said unto him, Father, I have sinned against heaven, and in thy sight, and am no more worthy to be called thy son.     21

But the father said to his servants, Bring forth the best robe, and put it on him; and put a ring on his hand, and shoes on his feet:     22

And bring hither the fatted calf, and kill it; and let us eat, and be merry:  23

For this my son was dead, and is alive again; he was lost, and is found. And they began to be merry.  24

Now his elder son was in the field: and as he came and drew nigh to the house, he heard musick and dancing.  25

And he called one of the servants, and asked what these things meant.  26

And he said unto him, Thy brother is come; and thy father hath killed the fatted calf, because he hath received him safe and sound.  27

And he was angry, and would not go in: therefore came his father out, and intreated him.  28

And he answering said to his father, Lo, these many years do I serve thee, neither transgressed I at any time thy commandment: and yet thou never gavest me a kid, that I might make merry with my friends:  29

But as soon as this thy son was come, which hath devoured thy living with harlots, thou hast killed for him the fatted calf.  30

And he said unto him, Son, thou art ever with me, and all that I have is thine.  31

It was meet that we should make merry, and be glad: for this thy brother was dead, and is alive again; and was lost, and is found.  32

There was a certain rich man, which had
a steward; and the same was accused unto
him that he had wasted his goods.

Lk 16: 1

And he called him, and said unto him,
How is it that I hear this of thee? give an
account of thy stewardship; for thou
mayest be no longer steward.

2

Then the steward said within himself,
What shall I do? for my lord taketh away
from me the stewardship: I cannot dig;
to beg I am ashamed.

3

I am resolved what to do, that, when I
am put out of the stewardship, they may
receive me into their houses.

4

So he called every one of his lord's debtors unto him, and said unto the first, How
much owest thou unto my lord?

5

And he said, An hundred measures of oil.
And he said unto him, Take thy bill, and
sit down quickly, and write fifty.

6

Then said he to another, And how much
owest thou? And he said, An hundred
measures of wheat. And he said unto him,
Take thy bill, and write fourscore.

7

And the lord commended the unjust steward, because he had done wisely: for the
children of this world are in their generation wiser than the children of light.

8

And I say unto you, Make to yourselves
friends of the mammon of unrighteousness; that, when ye fail, they may receive
you into everlasting habitations.

9

He that is faithful in that which is least is faithful also in much: and he that is unjust in the least is unjust also in much.

10

If therefore ye have not been faithful in the unrighteous mammon, who will commit to your trust the true riches?

11

And if ye have not been faithful in that which is another man's, who shall give you that which is your own?

12

No servant can serve two masters: for either he will hate the one, and love the other; or else he will hold to the one, and despise the other. Ye cannot serve God and mammon.

13

*The parable of the rich man and Lazarus, prefaced by Jesus' reproof to the Pharisees for their covetousness*

Ye are they which justify yourselves before men; but God knoweth your hearts: for that which is highly esteemed among men is abomination in the sight of God.

Lk 16:15

There was a certain rich man, which was clothed in purple and fine linen, and fared sumptuously every day:

19

And there was a certain beggar named Lazarus, which was laid at his gate, full of sores,

20

And desiring to be fed with the crumbs which fell from the rich man's table: moreover the dogs came and licked his sores.

21

And it came to pass, that the beggar died, and was carried by the angels into Abraham's bosom: the rich man also died, and was buried; 22

And in hell he lift up his eyes, being in torments, and seeth Abraham afar off, and Lazarus in his bosom. 23

And he cried and said, Father Abraham, have mercy on me, and send Lazarus, that he may dip the tip of his finger in water, and cool my tongue; for I am tormented in this flame. 24

But Abraham said, Son, remember that thou in thy lifetime receivedst thy good things, and likewise Lazarus evil things: but now he is comforted, and thou art tormented. 25

And beside all this, between us and you there is a great gulf fixed: so that they which would pass from hence to you cannot; neither can they pass to us, that would come from thence. 26

Then he said, I pray thee therefore, father, that thou wouldest send him to my father's house: 27

For I have five brethren; that he may testify unto them, lest they also come into this place of torment. 28

Abraham saith unto him, They have Moses and the prophets; let them hear them. 29

And he said, Nay, father Abraham: but if one went unto them from the dead, they will repent.

30

And he said unto him, If they hear not Moses and the prophets, neither will they be persuaded, though one rose from the dead.

31

Jesus teaches his disciples how to tell the works of duty from the works of faith.

If ye had faith as a grain of mustard seed, ye might say unto this sycamine tree, Be thou plucked up by the root, and be thou planted in the sea; and it should obey you.

Lk 17: 6

But which of you, having a servant plowing or feeding cattle, will say unto him by and by, when he is come from the field, Go and sit down to meat?

7

And will not rather say unto him, Make ready wherewith I may sup, and gird thyself, and serve me, till I have eaten and drunken; and afterward thou shalt eat and drink?

8

Doth he thank that servant because he did the things that were commanded him? I trow not.

9

So likewise ye, when ye shall have done all those things which are commanded you, say, We are unprofitable servants: we have done that which was our duty to do.

10

Jesus leaves the wilderness for Bethany to raise his friend Lazarus from the dead.

This sickness is not unto death, but for the glory of God, that the Son of God might be glorified thereby.

Jn 11: 4

Let us go into Judaea again.

7

Are there not twelve hours in the day? If any man walk in the day, he stumbleth not, because he seeth the light of this world.

9

But if a man walk in the night, he stumbleth, because there is no light in him.

10

Our friend Lazarus sleepeth; but I go, that I may awake him out of sleep.

11

Lazarus is dead.

14

And I am glad for your sakes that I was not there, to the intent ye may believe; nevertheless let us go unto him.

15

Thy brother shall rise again.

23

I am the resurrection, and the life: he that believeth in me, though he were dead, yet shall he live:

25

And whosoever liveth and believeth in me shall never die. Believest thou this?

26

Where have ye laid him?

34

Take ye away the stone.

39

Said I not unto thee, that, if thou wouldest believe, thou shouldest see the glory of God?  40

Father, I thank thee that thou hast heard me.  41

And I knew that thou hearest me always: but because of the people which stand by I said it, that they may believe that thou hast sent me.  42

Lazarus, come forth.  43

Loose him, and let him go.  44

As he journeys once more from town to town in Galilee, Jesus cleanses ten lepers, of whom only one, a Samaritan, returns to thank him.

Go shew yourselves unto the priests.  Lk 17:14

Were there not ten cleansed? but where are the nine?  17

There are not found that returned to give glory to God, save this stranger.  18

Arise, go thy way: thy faith hath made thee whole.  19

In answer to the Pharisees' question he foretells when and how God's kingdom will come.

The kingdom of God cometh not with observation:  Lk 17:20

Neither shall they say, Lo here! or, lo there! for, behold, the kingdom of God is within you.  21

The days will come, when ye shall desire to see one of the days of the Son of man, and ye shall not see it.   22

And they shall say to you, See here; or, see there: go not after them, nor follow them.   23

For as the lightning, that lighteneth out of the one part under heaven, shineth unto the other part under heaven; so shall also the Son of man be in his day.   24

But first must he suffer many things, and be rejected of this generation.   25

And as it was in the days of Noe, so shall it be also in the days of the Son of man.   26

They did eat, they drank, they married wives, they were given in marriage, until the day that Noe entered into the ark, and the flood came, and destroyed them all.   27

Likewise also as it was in the days of Lot; they did eat, they drank, they bought, they sold, they planted, they builded;   28

But the same day that Lot went out of Sodom it rained fire and brimstone from heaven, and destroyed them all.   29

Even thus shall it be in the day when the Son of man is revealed.   30

In that day, he which shall be upon the housetop, and his stuff in the house, let him not come down to take it away: and he that is in the field, let him likewise not return back.   31

Remember Lot's wife.   32

Whosoever shall seek to save his life shall lose it; and whosoever shall lose his life shall preserve it.

33

I tell you, in that night there shall be two men in one bed; the one shall be taken, and the other shall be left.

34

Two women shall be grinding together; the one shall be taken, and the other left.

35

Two men shall be in the field; the one shall be taken, and the other left.

36

Wheresoever the body is, thither will the eagles be gathered together.

37

To illustrate God's justice he tells the Pharisees two parables:

*The parable of the unjust judge*

There was in a city a judge, which feared not God, neither regarded man:

Lk 18: 2

And there was a widow in that city; and she came unto him, saying, Avenge me of mine adversary.

3

And he would not for a while: but afterward he said within himself, Though I fear not God, nor regard man;

4

Yet because this widow troubleth me, I will avenge her, lest by her continual coming she weary me.

5

Hear what the unjust judge saith.

6

And shall not God avenge his own elect, which cry day and night unto him, though he bear long with them?

7

I tell you that he will avenge them speedily. Nevertheless when the Son of man cometh, shall he find faith on the earth?

8

*The parable of the Pharisee and the publican*

Two men went up into the temple to pray; the one a Pharisee, and the other a publican.

Lk 18:10

The Pharisee stood and prayed thus with himself, God, I thank thee, that I am not as other men are, extortioners, unjust, adulterers, or even as this publican.

11

I fast twice in the week, I give tithes of all that I possess.

12

And the publican, standing afar off, would not lift up so much as his eyes unto heaven, but smote upon his breast, saying, God be merciful to me a sinner.

13

I tell you, this man went down to his house justified rather than the other: for every one that exalteth himself shall be abased; and he that humbleth himself shall be exalted.

14

*Jesus answers the Pharisees' questions about divorce.*

Have ye not read, that he which made them at the beginning made them male and female,

Mt 19: 4

And said, For this cause shall a man leave father and mother, and shall cleave to his wife: and they twain shall be one flesh?

5

Wherefore they are no more twain, but one flesh. What therefore God hath joined together, let not man put asunder.    6

Moses because of the hardness of your hearts suffered you to put away your wives: but from the beginning it was not so.    8

And I say unto you, Whosoever shall put away his wife, except it be for fornication, and shall marry another, committeth adultery: and whoso marrieth her which is put away doth commit adultery.    9

All men cannot receive this saying, save they to whom it is given.    11

For there are some eunuchs, which were so born from their mother's womb: and there are some eunuchs, which were made eunuchs of men: and there be eunuchs, which have made themselves eunuchs for the kingdom of heaven's sake. He that is able to receive it, let him receive it.    12

What did Moses command you?    Mk10:  3

For the hardness of your heart he wrote you this precept.    5

But from the beginning of the creation God made them male and female.    6

For this cause shall a man leave his father and mother, and cleave to his wife;    7

And they twain shall be one flesh: so then they are no more twain, but one flesh.    8

What therefore God hath joined together, let not man put asunder.    9

Whosoever shall put away his wife, and marry another, committeth adultery against her.

11

And if a woman shall put away her husband, and be married to another, she committeth adultery.

12

Jesus insists on receiving little children.

Suffer little children, and forbid them not, to come unto me: for of such is the kingdom of heaven.

Mt 19:14

Suffer the little children to come unto me, and forbid them not: for of such is the kingdom of God.

Mk10:14

Verily I say unto you, Whosoever shall not receive the kingdom of God as a little child, he shall not enter therein.

15

Suffer little children to come unto me, and forbid them not: for of such is the kingdom of God.

Lk 18:16

Verily I say unto you, Whosoever shall not receive the kingdom of God as a little child shall in no wise enter therein.

17

Jesus answers a rich young man's question about how to inherit eternal life.

Why callest thou me good? there is none good but one, that is, God: but if thou wilt enter into life, keep the commandments.

Mt 19:17

Thou shalt do no murder, Thou shalt not commit adultery, Thou shalt not steal, Thou shalt not bear false witness,    18

Honour thy father and thy mother: and, Thou shalt love thy neighbour as thyself.    19

If thou wilt be perfect, go and sell that thou hast, and give to the poor, and thou shalt have treasure in heaven: and come and follow me.    21

Verily I say unto you, That a rich man shall hardly enter into the kingdom of heaven.    23

And again I say unto you, It is easier for a camel to go through the eye of a needle, than for a rich man to enter into the kingdom of God.    24

With men this is impossible; but with God all things are possible.    26

Why callest thou me good? there is none good but one, that is, God.    Mk10:18

Thou knowest the commandments, Do not commit adultery, Do not kill, Do not steal, Do not bear false witness, Defraud not, Honour thy father and mother.    19

One thing thou lackest: go thy way, sell whatsoever thou hast, and give to the poor, and thou shalt have treasure in heaven: and come, take up the cross, and follow me.    21

How hardly shall they that have riches enter into the kingdom of God!    23

Children, how hard is it for them that trust in riches to enter into the kingdom of God!

24

It is easier for a camel to go through the eye of a needle, than for a rich man to enter into the kingdom of God.

25

With men it is impossible, but not with God: for with God all things are possible.

27

Why callest thou me good? none is good, save one, that is, God.

Lk 18:19

Thou knowest the commandments, Do not commit adultery, Do not kill, Do not steal, Do not bear false witness, Honour thy father and thy mother.

20

Yet lackest thou one thing: sell all that thou hast, and distribute unto the poor, and thou shalt have treasure in heaven: and come, follow me.

22

How hardly shall they that have riches enter into the kingdom of God!

24

For it is easier for a camel to go through a needle's eye, than for a rich man to enter into the kingdom of God.

25

The things which are impossible with men are possible with God.

27

Peter asks how the twelve disciples shall be rewarded.

Mt 19:28

Verily I say unto you, That ye which have followed me, in the regeneration when the Son of man shall sit in the throne of his glory, ye also shall sit upon twelve thrones, judging the twelve tribes of Israel.

### Related Saying

| | |
|---|---|
| Ye are they which have continued with me in my temptations. | Lk 22:28 |
| And I appoint unto you a kingdom, as my Father hath appointed unto me; | 29 |
| That ye may eat and drink at my table in my kingdom, and sit on thrones judging the twelve tribes of Israel. | 30 |

|  | Mt 19 [continued] |
|---|---|
| And every one that hath forsaken houses, or brethren, or sisters, or father, or mother, or wife, or children, or lands, for my name's sake, shall receive an hundredfold, and shall inherit everlasting life. | 29 |
| But many that are first shall be last; and the last shall be first. | 30 |

| | |
|---|---|
| Verily I say unto you, There is no man that hath left house, or brethren, or sisters, or father, or mother, or wife, or children, or lands, for my sake, and the gospel's, | Mk10:29 |
| But he shall receive an hundredfold now in this time, houses, and brethren, and sisters, and mothers, and children, and lands, with persecutions; and in the world to come eternal life. | 30 |
| But many that are first shall be last; and the last first. | 31 |

Verily I say unto you, There is no man that hath left house, or parents, or brethren, or wife, or children, for the kingdom of God's sake,

Lk 18:29

Who shall not receive manifold more in this present time, and in the world to come life everlasting.

30

Jesus illustrates his answer with the parable of the labourers in the vineyard.

For the kingdom of heaven is like unto a man that is an householder, which went out early in the morning to hire labourers into his vineyard.

Mt 20: 1

And when he had agreed with the labourers for a penny a day, he sent them into his vineyard.

2

And he went out about the third hour, and saw others standing idle in the marketplace,

3

And said unto them; Go ye also into the vineyard, and whatsoever is right I will give you. And they went their way.

4

Again he went out about the sixth and ninth hour, and did likewise.

5

And about the eleventh hour he went out, and found others standing idle, and saith unto them, Why stand ye here all the day idle?

6

They say unto him, Because no man hath hired us. He saith unto them, Go ye also into the vineyard; and whatsoever is right, that shall ye receive.

7

So when even was come, the lord of the vineyard saith unto his steward, Call the labourers, and give them their hire, beginning from the last unto the first.

8

And when they came that were hired about the eleventh hour, they received every man a penny.

9

But when the first came, they supposed that they should have received more; and they likewise received every man a penny.

10

And when they had received it, they murmured against the goodman of the house,

11

Saying, These last have wrought but one hour, and thou hast made them equal unto us, which have borne the burden and heat of the day.

12

But he answered one of them, and said, Friend, I do thee no wrong: didst not thou agree with me for a penny?

13

Take that thine is, and go thy way: I will give unto this last, even as unto thee.

14

Is it not lawful for me to do what I will with mine own? Is thine eye evil, because I am good?

15

So the last shall be first, and the first last: for many be called, but few chosen.

16

As he goes up to keep his last Passover in Jerusalem, Jesus foresees for the third time that he must die and rise again.

Behold, we go up to Jerusalem; and the Son of man shall be betrayed unto the chief priests and unto the scribes, and they shall condemn him to death,

Mt 20:18

And shall deliver him to the Gentiles to mock, and to scourge, and to crucify him: and the third day he shall rise again.

19

Behold, we go up to Jerusalem; and the Son of man shall be delivered unto the chief priests, and unto the scribes; and they shall condemn him to death, and shall deliver him to the Gentiles:

Mk10:33

And they shall mock him, and shall scourge him, and shall spit upon him, and shall kill him: and the third day he shall rise again.

34

Behold, we go up to Jerusalem, and all things that are written by the prophets concerning the Son of man shall be accomplished.

Lk 18:31

For he shall be delivered unto the Gentiles, and shall be mocked, and spitefully entreated, and spitted on:

32

And they shall scourge him, and put him to death: and the third day he shall rise again.

33

Jesus responds to
his disciples' claim
to share his glory.

What wilt thou?

Mt 20:21

Ye know not what ye ask. Are ye able to drink of the cup that I shall drink of, and to be baptized with the baptism that I am baptized with?

22

Ye shall drink indeed of my cup, and be baptized with the baptism that I am baptized with: but to sit on my right hand, and on my left, is not mine to give, but it shall be given to them for whom it is prepared of my Father.

23

Ye know that the princes of the Gentiles exercise dominion over them, and they that are great exercise authority upon them.

25

But it shall not be so among you: but whosoever will be great among you, let him be your minister;

26

And whosoever will be chief among you, let him be your servant:

27

Even as the Son of man came not to be ministered unto, but to minister, and to give his life a ransom for many.

28

What would ye that I should do for you?

Mk10:36

Ye know not what ye ask: can ye drink of the cup that I drink of? and be baptized with the baptism that I am baptized with?

38

Ye shall indeed drink of the cup that I
drink of; and with the baptism that I am
baptized withal shall ye be baptized:

39

But to sit on my right hand and on my
left hand is not mine to give; but it shall
be given to them for whom it is prepared.

40

Ye know that they which are accounted
to rule over the Gentiles exercise lordship
over them; and their great ones exercise
authority upon them.

42

But so shall it not be among you: but whosoever will be great among you, shall be
your minister:

43

And whosoever of you will be the chiefest,
shall be servant of all.

44

For even the Son of man came not to be
ministered unto, but to minister, and to
give his life a ransom for many.

45

*Related Saying*

The kings of the Gentiles exercise lordship over them; and they that exercise authority upon them are called benefactors.

Lk 22:25

But ye shall not be so: but he that is greatest among you, let him be as the younger;
and he that is chief, as he that doth serve.

26

For whether is greater, he that sitteth at
meat, or he that serveth? is not he that
sitteth at meat? but I am among you as
he that serveth.

27

At Jericho he heals
two blind men.

What will ye that I shall do unto you?

Mt 20:32

*Related Sayings*

What wilt thou that I should do unto thee?

Mk10:51

Go thy way; thy faith hath made thee whole.

52

What wilt thou that I shall do unto thee?

Lk 18:41

Receive thy sight: thy faith hath saved thee.

42

Jesus dines with the
rich publican Zac-
chaeus despite pro-
testations that Zac-
chaeus is a sinner.*

Zacchaeus, make haste, and come down;
for to day I must abide at thy house.

Lk 19: 5

This day is salvation come to this house,
forsomuch as he also is a son of Abraham.

9

For the Son of man is come to seek and to
save that which was lost.

10

Jesus sends his dis-
ciples to prepare his
entry into Jerusalem,
where the multitude
hails him as the
Christ.

Go into the village over against you, and
straightway ye shall find an ass tied, and a
colt with her: loose them, and bring them
unto me.

Mt 21: 2

---

* On this occasion Jesus tells the parable of the ten pounds cited under the parable
of the ten talents below.

And if any man say ought unto you, ye shall say, The Lord hath need of them; and straightway he will send them.

3

Go your way into the village over against you: and as soon as ye be entered into it, ye shall find a colt tied, whereon never man sat; loose him, and bring him.

Mk 11: 2

And if any man say unto you, Why do ye this? say ye that the Lord hath need of him; and straightway he will send him hither.

3

Go ye into the village over against you; in the which at your entering ye shall find a colt tied, whereon yet never man sat: loose him, and bring him hither.

Lk 19: 30

And if any man ask you, Why do ye loose him? thus shall ye say unto him, Because the Lord hath need of him.

31

I tell you that, if these should hold their peace, the stones would immediately cry out.

40

If thou hadst known, even thou, at least in this thy day, the things which belong unto thy peace! but now they are hid from thine eyes.

42

For the days shall come upon thee, that thine enemies shall cast a trench about thee, and compass thee round, and keep thee in on every side,

43

And shall lay thee even with the ground, and thy children within thee; and they shall not leave in thee one stone upon another;

44

because thou knewest not the time of thy visitation.

Various incidents occur shortly there-after: the cursing of the fig tree, the cleansing of the Temple and others.

It is written, My house shall be called the house of prayer; but ye have made it a den of thieves.

Mt 21:13

Yea; have ye never read, Out of the mouth of babes and sucklings thou hast perfected praise?

16

Let no fruit grow on thee henceforward for ever.

19

Verily I say unto you, If ye have faith, and doubt not, ye shall not only do this which is done to the fig tree, but also if ye shall say unto this mountain, Be thou removed, and be thou cast into the sea; it shall be done.

21

And all things, whatsoever ye shall ask in prayer, believing, ye shall receive.

22

No man eat fruit of thee hereafter for ever.

Mk 11:14

Is it not written, My house shall be called of all nations the house of prayer? but ye have made it a den of thieves.

17

It is written, My house is the house of prayer: but ye have made it a den of thieves.

Lk 19:46

*Related Sayings*

Take these things hence; make not my Father's house an house of merchandise.

Jn 2:16

Destroy this temple, and in three days I will raise it up.

19

Jesus expounds the lesson of the fig tree.

Have faith in God.

Mk 11:22

For verily I say unto you, That whosoever shall say unto this mountain, Be thou removed, and be thou cast into the sea; and shall not doubt in his heart, but shall believe that those things which he saith shall come to pass; he shall have whatsoever he saith.

23

Therefore I say unto you, What things soever ye desire, when ye pray, believe that ye receive them, and ye shall have them.

24

And when ye stand praying, forgive, if ye have ought against any: that your Father also which is in heaven may forgive you your trespasses.

25

But if ye do not forgive, neither will your Father which is in heaven forgive your trespasses.

26

The chief priests and Pharisees ask Jesus who empowered him to do his work.

I also will ask you one thing, which if ye tell me, I in like wise will tell you by what authority I do these things.

Mt 21:24

The baptism of John, whence was it? from heaven, or of men?

25

Neither tell I you by what authority I do these things.

27

I will also ask of you one question, and answer me, and I will tell you by what authority I do these things.

Mk 11:29

The baptism of John, was it from heaven, or of men? answer me.

30

Neither do I tell you by what authority I do these things.

33

I will also ask you one thing; and answer me:

Lk 20: 3

The baptism of John, was it from heaven, or of men?

4

Neither tell I you by what authority I do these things.

8

Jesus broadens his answer with parables:

*The parable of the sons*

But what think ye? A certain man had two sons; and he came to the first, and said, Son, go work to day in my vineyard.

Mt 21:28

He answered and said, I will not: but afterward he repented, and went.

29

And he came to the second, and said likewise. And he answered and said, I go, sir: and went not.

30

Whether of them twain did the will of his father? Verily I say unto you, That the publicans and the harlots go into the kingdom of God before you.

31

For John came unto you in the way of righteousness, and ye believed him not: but the publicans and the harlots believed him: and ye, when ye had seen it, repented not afterward, that ye might believe him.

32

*The parable of the unthankful husbandmen, with Jesus' interpretation*

Hear another parable: There was a certain householder, which planted a vineyard, and hedged it round about, and digged a winepress in it, and built a tower, and let it out to husbandmen, and went into a far country:

Mt 21:33

And when the time of the fruit drew near, he sent his servants to the husbandmen, that they might receive the fruits of it.

34

And the husbandmen took his servants, and beat one, and killed another, and stoned another.

35

Again, he sent other servants more than the first: and they did unto them likewise.

36

But last of all he sent unto them his son, saying, They will reverence my son.

37

But when the husbandmen saw the son, they said among themselves, This is the heir; come, let us kill him, and let us seize on his inheritance.

38

And they caught him, and cast him out
of the vineyard, and slew him.

39

When the lord therefore of the vineyard
cometh, what will he do unto those husbandmen?

40

Did ye never read in the scriptures, The
stone which the builders rejected, the same
is become the head of the corner: this is
the Lord's doing, and it is marvellous in
our eyes?

42

Therefore say I unto you, The kingdom
of God shall be taken from you, and given
to a nation bringing forth the fruits
thereof.

43

And whosoever shall fall on this stone shall
be broken: but on whomsoever it shall fall,
it will grind him to powder.

44

A certain man planted a vineyard, and set
an hedge about it, and digged a place for
the winefat, and built a tower, and let it
out to husbandmen, and went into a far
country.

Mk12: 1

And at the season he sent to the husbandmen a servant, that he might receive from
the husbandmen of the fruit of the vineyard.

2

And they caught him, and beat him, and
sent him away empty.

3

And again he sent unto them another servant; and at him they cast stones, and
wounded him in the head, and sent him
away shamefully handled.

4

And again he sent another; and him they killed, and many others; beating some, and killing some.     5

Having yet therefore one son, his wellbeloved, he sent him also last unto them, saying, They will reverence my son.     6

But those husbandmen said among themselves, This is the heir; come, let us kill him, and the inheritance shall be ours.     7

And they took him, and killed him, and cast him out of the vineyard.     8

What shall therefore the lord of the vineyard do? he will come and destroy the husbandmen, and will give the vineyard unto others.     9

And have ye not read this scripture; The stone which the builders rejected is become the head of the corner:     10

This was the Lord's doing, and it is marvellous in our eyes?     11

A certain man planted a vineyard, and let it forth to husbandmen, and went into a far country for a long time.     Lk 20: 9

And at the season he sent a servant to the husbandmen, that they should give him of the fruit of the vineyard: but the husbandmen beat him, and sent him away empty.     10

And again he sent another servant: and they beat him also, and entreated him shamefully, and sent him away empty.     11

And again he sent a third: and they wounded him also, and cast him out. 12

Then said the lord of the vineyard, What shall I do? I will send my beloved son: it may be they will reverence him when they see him. 13

But when the husbandmen saw him, they reasoned among themselves, saying, This is the heir: come, let us kill him, that the inheritance may be ours. 14

So they cast him out of the vineyard, and killed him. What therefore shall the lord of the vineyard do unto them? 15

He shall come and destroy these husbandmen, and shall give the vineyard to others. 16

What is this then that is written, The stone which the builders rejected, the same is become the head of the corner? 17

Whosoever shall fall upon that stone shall be broken; but on whomsoever it shall fall, it will grind him to powder. 18

*The parable of the royal marriage feast*

The kingdom of heaven is like unto a certain king, which made a marriage for his son, Mt 22: 2

And sent forth his servants to call them that were bidden to the wedding: and they would not come. 3

Again, he sent forth other servants, saying, Tell them which are bidden, Behold, 4

I have prepared my dinner: my oxen and my fatlings are killed, and all things are ready: come unto the marriage.

But they made light of it, and went their ways, one to his farm, another to his merchandise:  5

And the remnant took his servants, and entreated them spitefully, and slew them.  6

But when the king heard thereof, he was wroth: and he sent forth his armies, and destroyed those murderers, and burned up their city.  7

Then saith he to his servants, The wedding is ready, but they which were bidden were not worthy.  8

Go ye therefore into the highways, and as many as ye shall find, bid to the marriage.  9

So those servants went out into the highways, and gathered together all as many as they found, both bad and good: and the wedding was furnished with guests.  10

And when the king came in to see the guests, he saw there a man which had not on a wedding garment:  11

And he saith unto him, Friend, how camest thou in hither not having a wedding garment? And he was speechless.  12

Then said the king to the servants, Bind him hand and foot, and take him away, and cast him into outer darkness; there shall be weeping and gnashing of teeth.  13

For many are called, but few are chosen.  14

*Related Sayings*

When thou art bidden of any man to a wedding, sit not down in the highest room; lest a more honourable man than thou be bidden of him;

Lk 14: 8

And he that bade thee and him come and say to thee, Give this man place; and thou begin with shame to take the lowest room.

9

But when thou art bidden, go and sit down in the lowest room; that when he that bade thee cometh, he may say unto thee, Friend, go up higher: then shalt thou have worship in the presence of them that sit at meat with thee.

10

For whosoever exalteth himself shall be abased; and he that humbleth himself shall be exalted.

11

When thou makest a dinner or a supper, call not thy friends, nor thy brethren, neither thy kinsmen, nor thy rich neighbours; lest they also bid thee again, and a recompence be made thee.

12

But when thou makest a feast, call the poor, the maimed, the lame, the blind:

13

And thou shalt be blessed; for they cannot recompense thee: for thou shalt be recompensed at the resurrection of the just.

14

A certain man made a great supper, and bade many:

16

And sent his servant at supper time to say to them that were bidden, Come; for all things are now ready.

17

And they all with one consent began to make excuse. The first said unto him, I have bought a piece of ground, and I must needs go and see it: I pray thee have me excused.   18

And another said, I have bought five yoke of oxen, and I go to prove them: I pray thee have me excused.   19

And another said, I have married a wife, and therefore I cannot come.   20

So that servant came, and shewed his lord these things. Then the master of the house being angry said to his servant, Go out quickly into the streets and lanes of the city, and bring in hither the poor, and the maimed, and the halt, and the blind.   21

And the servant said, Lord, it is done as thou hast commanded, and yet there is room.   22

And the lord said unto the servant, Go out into the highways and hedges, and compel them to come in, that my house may be filled.   23

For I say unto you, That none of those men which were bidden shall taste of my supper.   24

Pharisees and Herodians ask Jesus whether it be right to pay tribute to Caesar.

Why tempt ye me, ye hypocrites?   Mt 22:18

Shew me the tribute money.   19

Whose is this image and superscription?   20

Render therefore unto Caesar the things which are Caesar's; and unto God the things that are God's.   21

Why tempt ye me? bring me a penny, that I may see it.

Mk12:15

Whose is this image and superscription?

16

Render to Caesar the things that are Caesar's, and to God the things that are God's.

17

Why tempt ye me?

Lk 20:23

Shew me a penny. Whose image and superscription hath it?

24

Render therefore unto Caesar the things which be Caesar's, and unto God the things which be God's.

25

He refutes the Saducees' arguments against the resurrection.

Ye do err, not knowing the scriptures, nor the power of God.

Mt 22:29

For in the resurrection they neither marry, nor are given in marriage, but are as the angels of God in heaven.

30

But as touching the resurrection of the dead, have ye not read that which was spoken unto you by God, saying,

31

I am the God of Abraham, and the God of Isaac, and the God of Jacob? God is not the God of the dead, but of the living.

32

Do ye not therefore err, because ye know not the scriptures, neither the power of God?

Mk12:24

For when they shall rise from the dead, they neither marry, nor are given in marriage; but are as the angels which are in heaven.

25

And as touching the dead, that they rise: have ye not read in the book of Moses, how in the bush God spake unto him, saying, I am the God of Abraham, and the God of Isaac, and the God of Jacob?

26

He is not the God of the dead, but the God of the living: ye therefore do greatly err.

27

The children of this world marry, and are given in marriage:

Lk 20:34

But they which shall be accounted worthy to obtain that world, and the resurrection from the dead, neither marry, nor are given in marriage:

35

Neither can they die any more: for they are equal unto the angels; and are the children of God, being the children of the resurrection.

36

Now that the dead are raised, even Moses shewed at the bush, when he calleth the Lord the God of Abraham, and the God of Isaac, and the God of Jacob.

37

For he is not a God of the dead, but of the living: for all live unto him.

38

A scribe among them asks Jesus which is the first and greatest commandment.

Thou shalt love the Lord thy God with all thy heart, and with all thy soul, and with all thy mind.

Mt 22:37

This is the first and great commandment. 38

And the second is like unto it, Thou shalt love thy neighbour as thyself. 39

On these two commandments hang all the law and the prophets. 40

The first of all the commandments is, Hear, O Israel; The Lord our God is one Lord: Mk12:29

And thou shalt love the Lord thy God with all thy heart, and with all thy soul, and with all thy mind, and with all thy strength: this is the first commandment. 30

And the second is like, namely this, Thou shalt love thy neighbour as thyself. There is none other commandment greater than these. 31

Thou art not far from the kingdom of God. 34

He refutes the Pharisees' conception of the Christ and rebukes them for their practices.

What think ye of Christ? whose son is he? Mt 22:42

How then doth David in spirit call him Lord, saying, 43

The LORD said unto my Lord, Sit thou on my right hand, till I make thine enemies thy footstool? 44

If David then call him Lord, how is he his son? 45

How say the scribes that Christ is the Son of David?

Mk12:35

For David himself said by the Holy Ghost, The LORD said to my Lord, Sit thou on my right hand, till I make thine enemies thy footstool.

36

David therefore himself calleth him Lord; and whence is he then his son?

37

Beware of the scribes, which love to go in long clothing, and love salutations in the marketplaces,

38

And the chief seats in the synagogues, and the uppermost rooms at feasts:

39

Which devour widows' houses, and for a pretence make long prayers: these shall receive greater damnation.

40

How say they that Christ is David's son?

Lk 20:41

And David himself saith in the book of Psalms, The LORD said unto my Lord, Sit thou on my right hand,

42

Till I make thine enemies thy footstool.

43

David therefore calleth him Lord, how is he then his son?

44

Beware of the scribes, which desire to walk in long robes, and love greetings in the markets, and the highest seats in the synagogues, and the chief rooms at feasts;

46

Which devour widows' houses, and for a shew make long prayers: the same shall receive greater damnation.

47

Jesus commends a poor widow's generosity.

Verily I say unto you, That this poor widow hath cast more in, than all they which have cast into the treasury:

Mk12:43

For all they did cast in of their abundance; but she of her want did cast in all that she had, even all her living.

44

Of a truth I say unto you, that this poor widow hath cast in more than they all:

Lk 21: 3

For all these have of their abundance cast in unto the offerings of God: but she of her penury hath cast in all the living that she had.

4

Jesus laments over the Pharisees' hypocrisy and over Jerusalem.

The scribes and the Pharisees sit in Moses' seat:

Mt 23: 2

All therefore whatsoever they bid you observe, that observe and do; but do not ye after their works: for they say, and do not.

3

For they bind heavy burdens and grievous to be borne, and lay them on men's shoulders; but they themselves will not move them with one of their fingers.

4

But all their works they do for to be seen of men: they make broad their phylacteries, and enlarge the borders of their garments,

5

And love the uppermost rooms at feasts, and the chief seats in the synagogues,   6

And greetings in the markets, and to be called of men, Rabbi, Rabbi.   7

But be not ye called Rabbi: for one is your Master, even Christ; and all ye are brethren.   8

And call no man your father upon the earth: for one is your Father, which is in heaven.   9

Neither be ye called masters: for one is your Master, even Christ.   10

But he that is greatest among you shall be your servant.   11

And whosoever shall exalt himself shall be abased; and he that shall humble himself shall be exalted.   12

But woe unto you, scribes and Pharisees, hypocrites! for ye shut up the kingdom of heaven against men: for ye neither go in yourselves, neither suffer ye them that are entering to go in.   13

Woe unto you, scribes and Pharisees, hypocrites! for ye devour widows' houses, and for a pretence make long prayer: therefore ye shall receive the greater damnation.   14

Woe unto you, scribes and Pharisees, hypocrites! for ye compass sea and land to make one proselyte, and when he is made, ye make him twofold more the child of hell than yourselves.   15

Woe unto you, ye blind guides, which say, 16
Whosoever shall swear by the temple, it
is nothing; but whosoever shall swear by
the gold of the temple, he is a debtor!

Ye fools and blind: for whether is greater, 17
the gold, or the temple that sanctifieth the
gold?

And, Whosoever shall swear by the altar, 18
it is nothing; but whosoever sweareth by
the gift that is upon it, he is guilty.

Ye fools and blind: for whether is greater, 19
the gift, or the altar that sanctifieth the
gift?

Whoso therefore shall swear by the altar, 20
sweareth by it, and by all things thereon.

And whoso shall swear by the temple, 21
sweareth by it, and by him that dwelleth
therein.

And he that shall swear by heaven, 22
sweareth by the throne of God, and by
him that sitteth thereon.

Woe unto you, scribes and Pharisees, 23
hypocrites! for ye pay tithe of mint and
anise and cummin, and have omitted the
weightier matters of the law, judgment,
mercy, and faith: these ought ye to have
done, and not to leave the other undone.

Ye blind guides, which strain at a gnat, 24
and swallow a camel.

Woe unto you, scribes and Pharisees, 25
hypocrites! for ye make clean the outside
of the cup and of the platter, but within
they are full of extortion and excess.

Thou blind Pharisee, cleanse first that 26
which is within the cup and platter, that
the outside of them may be clean also.

Woe unto you, scribes and Pharisees, 27
hypocrites! for ye are like unto whited sepulchres, which indeed appear beautiful
outward, but are within full of dead men's
bones, and of all uncleanness.

Even so ye also outwardly appear righteous 28
unto men, but within ye are full of hypocrisy and iniquity.

Woe unto you, scribes and Pharisees, 29
hypocrites! because ye build the tombs of
the prophets, and garnish the sepulchres
of the righteous,

And say, If we had been in the days of our 30
fathers, we would not have been partak-
ers with them in the blood of the prophets.

Wherefore ye be witnesses unto your- 31
selves, that ye are the children of them
which killed the prophets.

Fill ye up then the measure of your fa- 32
thers.

Ye serpents, ye generation of vipers, how 33
can ye escape the damnation of hell?

Wherefore, behold, I send unto you 34
prophets, and wise men, and scribes: and
some of them ye shall kill and crucify; and
some of them shall ye scourge in your
synagogues, and persecute them from city
to city:

That upon you may come all the righteous blood shed upon the earth, from the
blood of righteous Abel unto the blood
of Zacharias son of Barachias, whom ye
slew between the temple and the altar.

35

Verily I say unto you, All these things shall
come upon this generation.

36

O Jerusalem, Jerusalem, thou that killest
the prophets, and stonest them which are
sent unto thee, how often would I have
gathered thy children together, even as a
hen gathereth her chickens under her
wings, and ye would not!

37

Behold, your house is left unto you desolate.

38

For I say unto you, Ye shall not see me
henceforth, till ye shall say, Blessed is he
that cometh in the name of the Lord.

39

### Related Saying

O Jerusalem, Jerusalem, which killest the
prophets, and stonest them that are sent
unto thee; how often would I have gathered thy children together, as a hen doth
gather her brood under her wings, and ye
would not!

Lk 13:34

Behold, your house is left unto you desolate: and verily I say unto you, Ye shall
not see me, until the time come when ye
shall say, Blessed is he that cometh in the
name of the Lord.

35

Jesus interprets his death to certain Greeks and to the people in the Temple.

The hour is come, that the Son of man should be glorified.

Jn 12:23

Verily, verily, I say unto you, Except a corn of wheat fall into the ground and die, it abideth alone: but if it die, it bringeth forth much fruit.

24

He that loveth his life shall lose it; and he that hateth his life in this world shall keep it unto life eternal.

25

If any man serve me, let him follow me; and where I am, there shall also my servant be: if any man serve me, him will my Father honour.

26

Now is my soul troubled; and what shall I say? Father, save me from this hour: but for this cause came I unto this hour.

27

Father, glorify thy name.

28

This voice came not because of me, but for your sakes.

30

Now is the judgment of this world: now shall the prince of this world be cast out.

31

And I, if I be lifted up from the earth, will draw all men unto me.

32

Yet a little while is the light with you. Walk while ye have the light, lest darkness come upon you: for he that walketh in darkness knoweth not whither he goeth.

35

While ye have light, believe in the light, that ye may be the children of light.

36

He that believeth on me, believeth not on me, but on him that sent me.

44

And he that seeth me seeth him that sent me.

45

I am come a light into the world, that whosoever believeth on me should not abide in darkness.

46

And if any man hear my words, and believe not, I judge him not: for I came not to judge the world, but to save the world.

47

He that rejecteth me, and receiveth not my words, hath one that judgeth him: the word that I have spoken, the same shall judge him in the last day.

48

For I have not spoken of myself; but the Father which sent me, he gave me a commandment, what I should say, and what I should speak.

49

And I know that his commandment is life everlasting: whatsoever I speak therefore, even as the Father said unto me, so I speak.

50

Jesus foretells the destruction of the Temple and the coming of the Son of Man at the end of the world.

Mt 24: 2

See ye not all these things? verily I say unto you, There shall not be left here one stone upon another, that shall not be thrown down.

Take heed that no man deceive you.                4

For many shall come in my name, say-             5
ing, I am Christ; and shall deceive many.

And ye shall hear of wars and rumours of         6
wars: see that ye be not troubled: for all
these things must come to pass, but the
end is not yet.

For nation shall rise against nation, and        7
kingdom against kingdom: and there shall
be famines, and pestilences, and earthquakes, in divers places.

All these are the beginning of sorrows.          8

Then shall they deliver you up to be af-          9
flicted, and shall kill you: and ye shall be
hated of all nations for my name's sake.

And then shall many be offended, and             10
shall betray one another, and shall hate
one another.

And many false prophets shall rise, and          11
shall deceive many.

And because iniquity shall abound, the           12
love of many shall wax cold.

But he that shall endure unto the end, the       13
same shall be saved.

And this gospel of the kingdom shall be          14
preached in all the world for a witness
unto all nations; and then shall the end
come.

When ye therefore shall see the abomina-         15
tion of desolation, spoken of by Daniel
the prophet, stand in the holy place,

Then let them which be in Judaea flee into the mountains:  16

Let him which is on the housetop not come down to take any thing out of his house:  17

Neither let him which is in the field return back to take his clothes.  18

And woe unto them that are with child, and to them that give suck in those days!  19

But pray ye that your flight be not in the winter, neither on the sabbath day:  20

For then shall be great tribulation, such as was not since the beginning of the world to this time, no, nor ever shall be.  21

And except those days should be shortened, there should no flesh be saved: but for the elect's sake those days shall be shortened.  22

Then if any man shall say unto you, Lo, here is Christ, or there; believe it not.  23

For there shall arise false Christs, and false prophets, and shall shew great signs and wonders; insomuch that, if it were possible, they shall deceive the very elect.  24

Behold, I have told you before.  25

Wherefore if they shall say unto you, Behold, he is in the desert; go not forth: behold, he is in the secret chambers; believe it not.  26

For as the lightning cometh out of the east, and shineth even unto the west; so shall also the coming of the Son of man be.  27

For wheresoever the carcase is, there will the eagles be gathered together. | 28

Immediately after the tribulation of those days shall the sun be darkened, and the moon shall not give her light, and the stars shall fall from heaven, and the powers of the heavens shall be shaken: | 29

And then shall appear the sign of the Son of man in heaven: and then shall all the tribes of the earth mourn, and they shall see the Son of man coming in the clouds of heaven with power and great glory. | 30

And he shall send his angels with a great sound of a trumpet, and they shall gather together his elect from the four winds, from one end of heaven to the other. | 31

Now learn a parable of the fig tree; When his branch is yet tender, and putteth forth leaves, ye know that summer is nigh: | 32

So likewise ye, when ye shall see all these things, know that it is near, even at the doors. | 33

Verily I say unto you, This generation shall not pass, till all these things be fulfilled. | 34

Heaven and earth shall pass away, but my words shall not pass away. | 35

But of that day and hour knoweth no man, no, not the angels of heaven, but my Father only. | 36

But as the days of Noe were, so shall also the coming of the Son of man be. | 37

For as in the days that were before the flood they were eating and drinking, marrying and | 38 giving in marriage, until the day that Noe entered into the ark,

And knew not until the flood came, and took them all away; so shall also the coming of the Son of man be.                    39

Then shall two be in the field; the one shall be taken, and the other left.                    40

Two women shall be grinding at the mill; the one shall be taken, and the other left.                    41

Seest thou these great buildings? there shall not be left one stone upon another, that shall not be thrown down.                    Mk13: 2

Take heed lest any man deceive you:                    5

For many shall come in my name, saying, I am Christ; and shall deceive many.                    6

And when ye shall hear of wars and rumours of wars, be ye not troubled: for such things must needs be; but the end shall not be yet.                    7

For nation shall rise against nation, and kingdom against kingdom: and there shall be earthquakes in divers places, and there shall be famines and troubles: these are the beginnings of sorrows.                    8

But take heed to yourselves: for they shall deliver you up to councils; and in the synagogues ye shall be beaten: and ye shall be brought before rulers and kings for my sake, for a testimony against them.                    9

And the gospel must first be published among all nations.                    10

But when they shall lead you, and deliver
you up, take no thought beforehand what
ye shall speak, neither do ye premeditate:
but whatsoever shall be given you in that
hour, that speak ye: for it is not ye that
speak, but the Holy Ghost.

11

Now the brother shall betray the brother
to death, and the father the son; and children shall rise up against their parents, and
shall cause them to be put to death.

12

And ye shall be hated of all men for my
name's sake: but he that shall endure unto
the end, the same shall be saved.

13

But when ye shall see the abomination of
desolation, spoken of by Daniel the
prophet, standing where it ought not,
then let them that be in Judaea flee to the
mountains:

14

And let him that is on the housetop not
go down into the house, neither enter
therein, to take any thing out of his house:

15

And let him that is in the field not turn
back again for to take up his garment.

16

But woe to them that are with child, and
to them that give suck in those days!

17

And pray ye that your flight be not in the
winter.

18

For in those days shall be affliction, such
as was not from the beginning of the creation which God created unto this time,
neither shall be.

19

And except that the Lord had shortened
those days, no flesh should be saved: but

20

for the elect's sake, whom he hath chosen, he hath shortened the days.

And then if any man shall say to you, Lo,          21
here is Christ; or, lo, he is there; believe
him not:

For false Christs and false prophets shall          22
rise, and shall shew signs and wonders, to
seduce, if it were possible, even the elect.

But take ye heed: behold, I have foretold          23
you all things.

But in those days, after that tribulation,          24
the sun shall be darkened, and the moon
shall not give her light,

And the stars of heaven shall fall, and the          25
powers that are in heaven shall be shaken.

And then shall they see the Son of man          26
coming in the clouds with great power
and glory.

And then shall he send his angels, and          27
shall gather together his elect from the four
winds, from the uttermost part of the
earth to the uttermost part of heaven.

Now learn a parable of the fig tree; When          28
her branch is yet tender, and putteth forth
leaves, ye know that summer is near:

So ye in like manner, when ye shall see          29
these things come to pass, know that it is
nigh, even at the doors.

Verily I say unto you, that this generation          30
shall not pass, till all these things be done.

Heaven and earth shall pass away: but my          31
words shall not pass away.

But of that day and that hour knoweth no man, no, not the angels which are in heaven, neither the Son, but the Father. **32**

Take ye heed, watch and pray: for ye know not when the time is. **33**

For the Son of man is as a man taking a far journey, who left his house, and gave authority to his servants, and to every man his work, and commanded the porter to watch. **34**

Watch ye therefore: for ye know not when the master of the house cometh, at even, or at midnight, or at the cock-crowing, or in the morning: **35**

Lest coming suddenly he find you sleeping. **36**

And what I say unto you I say unto all, Watch. **37**

As for these things which ye behold, the days will come, in the which there shall not be left one stone upon another, that shall not be thrown down. **Lk 21: 6**

Take heed that ye be not deceived: for many shall come in my name, saying, I am Christ; and the time draweth near: go ye not therefore after them. **8**

But when ye shall hear of wars and commotions, be not terrified: for these things must first come to pass; but the end is not by and by. **9**

Nation shall rise against nation, and kingdom against kingdom: 10

And great earthquakes shall be in divers places, and famines, and pestilences; and fearful sights and great signs shall there be from heaven. 11

But before all these, they shall lay their hands on you, and persecute you, delivering you up to the synagogues, and into prisons, being brought before kings and rulers for my name's sake. 12

And it shall turn to you for a testimony. 13

Settle it therefore in your hearts, not to meditate before what ye shall answer: 14

For I will give you a mouth and wisdom, which all your adversaries shall not be able to gainsay nor resist. 15

And ye shall be betrayed both by parents, and brethren, and kinsfolks, and friends; and some of you shall they cause to be put to death. 16

And ye shall be hated of all men for my name's sake. 17

But there shall not an hair of your head perish. 18

In your patience possess ye your souls. 19

And when ye shall see Jerusalem compassed with armies, then know that the desolation thereof is nigh. 20

Then let them which are in Judaea flee to the mountains; and let them which are in 21 the midst of it depart out; and let not them that are in the countries enter thereinto.

For these be the days of vengeance, that all things which are written may be fulfilled. 22

But woe unto them that are with child, and to them that give suck, in those days! for there shall be great distress in the land, and wrath upon this people. 23

And they shall fall by the edge of the sword, and shall be led away captive into all nations: and Jerusalem shall be trodden down of the Gentiles, until the times of the Gentiles be fulfilled. 24

And there shall be signs in the sun, and in the moon, and in the stars; and upon the earth distress of nations, with perplexity; the sea and the waves roaring; 25

Men's hearts failing them for fear, and for looking after those things which are coming on the earth: for the powers of heaven shall be shaken. 26

And then shall they see the Son of man coming in a cloud with power and great glory. 27

And when these things begin to come to pass, then look up, and lift up your heads; for your redemption draweth nigh. 28

Behold the fig tree, and all the trees; 29

When they now shoot forth, ye see and know of your own selves that summer is now nigh at hand. 30

So likewise ye, when ye see these things come to pass, know ye that the kingdom of God is nigh at hand.

31

Verily I say unto you, This generation shall not pass away, till all be fulfilled.

32

Heaven and earth shall pass away: but my words shall not pass away.

33

And take heed to yourselves, lest at any time your hearts be overcharged with surfeiting, and drunkenness, and cares of this life, and so that day come upon you unawares.

34

For as a snare shall it come on all them that dwell on the face of the whole earth.

35

Watch ye therefore, and pray always, that ye may be accounted worthy to escape all these things that shall come to pass, and to stand before the Son of man.

36

Jesus foretells the coming of the Son of Man in parables:

*The parable of the watchful householder*

Watch therefore: for ye know not what hour your Lord doth come.

Mt 24:42

But know this, that if the goodman of the house had known in what watch the thief would come, he would have watched, and would not have suffered his house to be broken up.

43

Therefore be ye also ready: for in such an hour as ye think not the Son of man cometh.

44

And this know, that if the goodman of the house had known what hour the thief would come, he would have watched, and not have suffered his house to be broken through.

Lk 12:39

Be ye therefore ready also: for the Son of man cometh at an hour when ye think not.

40

*The parable of the faithful and wise servant*

Who then is a faithful and wise servant, whom his lord hath made ruler over his household, to give them meat in due season?

Mt 24:45

Blessed is that servant, whom his lord when he cometh shall find so doing.

46

Verily I say unto you, That he shall make him ruler over all his goods.

47

But and if that evil servant shall say in his heart, My lord delayeth his coming;

48

And shall begin to smite his fellow-servants, and to eat and drink with the drunken;

49

The lord of that servant shall come in a day when he looketh not for him, and in an hour that he is not aware of,

50

And shall cut him asunder, and appoint him his portion with the hypocrites: there shall be weeping and gnashing of teeth.

51

Who then is that faithful and wise steward, whom his lord shall make ruler over his household, to give them their portion of meat in due season?

Lk 12:42

Blessed is that servant, whom his lord when he cometh shall find so doing.

43

Of a truth I say unto you, that he will make him ruler over all that he hath.

44

But and if that servant say in his heart, My lord delayeth his coming; and shall begin to beat the menservants and maidens, and to eat and drink, and to be drunken;

45

The lord of that servant will come in a day when he looketh not for him, and at an hour when he is not aware, and will cut him in sunder, and will appoint him his portion with the unbelievers.

46

And that servant, which knew his lord's will, and prepared not himself, neither did according to his will, shall be beaten with many stripes.

47

But he that knew not, and did commit things worthy of stripes, shall be beaten with few stripes. For unto whomsoever much is given, of him shall be much required: and to whom men have committed much, of him they will ask the more.

48

*The parable of the ten virgins*

Then shall the kingdom of heaven be likened unto ten virgins, which took their

Mt 25: 1

lamps, and went forth to meet the bridegroom.

And five of them were wise, and five were
foolish.                                                    2

They that were foolish took their lamps,                    3
and took no oil with them:

But the wise took oil in their vessels with                 4
their lamps.

While the bridegroom tarried, they all                      5
slumbered and slept.

And at midnight there was a cry made,                       6
Behold, the bridegroom cometh; go ye out
to meet him.

Then all those virgins arose, and trimmed                   7
their lamps.

And the foolish said unto the wise, Give                    8
us of your oil; for our lamps are gone out.

But the wise answered, saying, Not so; lest                 9
there be not enough for us and you: but
go ye rather to them that sell, and buy for
yourselves.

And while they went to buy, the bride-                     10
groom came; and they that were ready
went in with him to the marriage: and
the door was shut.

Afterward came also the other virgins, say-                11
ing, Lord, Lord, open to us.

But he answered and said, Verily I say unto                12
you, I know you not.

*Related Saying*

When once the master of the house is risen up, and hath shut to the door, and ye begin to stand without, and to knock at the door, saying, Lord, Lord, open unto us; and he shall answer and say unto you, I know you not whence ye are.

Lk 13:25

Watch therefore, for ye know neither the day nor the hour wherein the Son of man cometh.

Mt 25 [continued]
13

Let your loins be girded about, and your lights burning;

Lk 12:35

And ye yourselves like unto men that wait for their lord, when he will return from the wedding; that when he cometh and knocketh, they may open unto him immediately.

36

Blessed are those servants, whom the lord when he cometh shall find watching: verily I say unto you, that he shall gird himself, and make them to sit down to meat, and will come forth and serve them.

37

And if he shall come in the second watch, or come in the third watch, and find them so, blessed are those servants.

38

*The parable of the ten talents*

For the kingdom of heaven is as a man travelling into a far country, who called his own servants, and delivered unto them his goods.

Mt 25:14

And unto one he gave five talents, to another two, and to another one; to every man according to his several ability; and straightway took his journey.

15

Then he that had received the five talents went and traded with the same, and made them other five talents.

16

And likewise he that had received two, he also gained other two.

17

But he that had received one went and digged in the earth, and hid his lord's money.

18

After a long time the lord of those servants cometh, and reckoneth with them.

19

And so he that had received five talents came and brought other five talents, saying, Lord, thou deliveredst unto me five talents: behold, I have gained beside them five talents more.

20

His lord said unto him, Well done, thou good and faithful servant: thou hast been faithful over a few things, I will make thee ruler over many things: enter thou into the joy of thy lord.

21

He also that had received two talents came and said, Lord, thou deliveredst unto me two talents: behold, I have gained two other talents beside them.

22

His lord said unto him, Well done, good and faithful servant; thou hast been faithful over a few things, I will make thee ruler over many things: enter thou into the joy of thy lord.

23

Then he which had received the one talent came and said, Lord, I knew thee that
thou art an hard man, reaping where thou
hast not sown, and gathering where thou
hast not strawed:

24

And I was afraid, and went and hid thy
talent in the earth: lo, there thou hast that
is thine.

25

His lord answered and said unto him,
Thou wicked and slothful servant, thou
knewest that I reap where I sowed not,
and gather where I have not strawed:

26

Thou oughtest therefore to have put my
money to the exchangers, and then at my
coming I should have received mine own
with usury.

27

Take therefore the talent from him, and
give it unto him which hath ten talents.

28

For unto every one that hath shall be
given, and he shall have abundance: but
from him that hath not shall be taken
away even that which he hath.

29

And cast ye the unprofitable servant into
outer darkness: there shall be weeping and
gnashing of teeth.

30

### Related Saying

A certain nobleman went into a far country to receive for himself a kingdom, and
to return.

Lk 19:12

And he called his ten servants, and delivered them ten pounds, and said unto
them, Occupy till I come.

13

But his citizens hated him, and sent a message after him, saying, We will not have this man to reign over us.

14

And it came to pass, that when he was returned, having received the kingdom, then he commanded these servants to be called unto him, to whom he had given the money, that he might know how much every man had gained by trading.

15

Then came the first, saying, Lord, thy pound hath gained ten pounds.

16

And he said unto him, Well, thou good servant: because thou hast been faithful in a very little, have thou authority over ten cities.

17

And the second came, saying, Lord, thy pound hath gained five pounds.

18

And he said likewise to him, Be thou also over five cities.

19

And another came, saying, Lord, behold, here is thy pound, which I have kept laid up in a napkin:

20

For I feared thee, because thou art an austere man: thou takest up that thou layedst not down, and reapest that thou didst not sow.

21

And he saith unto him, Out of thine own mouth will I judge thee, thou wicked servant. Thou knewest that I was an austere man, taking up that I laid not down, and reaping that I did not sow:

22

Wherefore then gavest not thou my money into the bank, that at my coming I might have required mine own with usury?

*23*

And he said unto them that stood by, Take from him the pound, and give it to him that hath ten pounds.

*24*

(And they said unto him, Lord, he hath ten pounds.)

*25*

For I say unto you, That unto every one which hath shall be given; and from him that hath not, even that he hath shall be taken away from him.

*26*

But those mine enemies, which would not that I should reign over them, bring hither, and slay them before me.

*27*

**Jesus envisions the last judgment.**

When the Son of man shall come in his glory, and all the holy angels with him, then shall he sit upon the throne of his glory:

Mt 25:31

And before him shall be gathered all nations: and he shall separate them one from another, as a shepherd divideth his sheep from the goats:

*32*

And he shall set the sheep on his right hand, but the goats on the left.

*33*

Then shall the King say unto them on his right hand, Come, ye blessed of my Father, inherit the kingdom prepared for you from the foundation of the world:

*34*

For I was an hungred, and ye gave me meat: I was thirsty, and ye gave me drink: I was a stranger, and ye took me in:   35

Naked, and ye clothed me: I was sick, and ye visited me: I was in prison, and ye came unto me.   36

Then shall the righteous answer him, saying, Lord, when saw we thee an hungred, and fed thee? or thirsty, and gave thee drink?   37

When saw we thee a stranger, and took thee in? or naked, and clothed thee?   38

Or when saw we thee sick, or in prison, and came unto thee?   39

And the King shall answer and say unto them, Verily I say unto you, Inasmuch as ye have done it unto one of the least of these my brethren, ye have done it unto me.   40

Then shall he say also unto them on the left hand, Depart from me, ye cursed, into everlasting fire, prepared for the devil and his angels:   41

For I was an hungred, and ye gave me no meat: I was thirsty, and ye gave me no drink:   42

I was a stranger, and ye took me not in: naked, and ye clothed me not: sick, and in prison, and ye visited me not.   43

Then shall they also answer him, saying, Lord, when saw we thee an hungred, or athirst, or a stranger, or naked, or sick, or in prison, and did not minister unto thee?   44

Then shall he answer them, saying, Verily I say unto you, Inasmuch as ye did it not to one of the least of these, ye did it not to me.

45

And these shall go away into everlasting punishment: but the righteous into life eternal.

46

He foresees his betrayal and crucifixion at the Passover.

Ye know that after two days is the feast of the passover, and the Son of man is betrayed to be crucified.

Mt 26: 2

At supper in Bethany Jesus is anointed with costly ointment by a woman whose act he defends against the objections of others.

Why trouble ye the woman? for she hath wrought a good work upon me.

Mt 26:10

For ye have the poor always with you; but me ye have not always.

11

For in that she hath poured this ointment on my body, she did it for my burial.

12

Verily I say unto you, Wheresoever this gospel shall be preached in the whole world, there shall also this, that this woman hath done, be told for a memorial of her.

13

Let her alone; why trouble ye her? she hath wrought a good work on me.

Mk14: 6

For ye have the poor with you always, and whensoever ye will ye may do them good: but me ye have not always.

7

She hath done what she could: she is come aforehand to anoint my body to the burying.

8

Verily I say unto you, Wheresoever this gospel shall be preached throughout the whole world, this also that she hath done shall be spoken of for a memorial of her.

9

Let her alone: against the day of my burying hath she kept this.

Jn 12: 7

For the poor always ye have with you; but me ye have not always.

8

*Related Saying*

Simon, I have somewhat to say unto thee.

Lk 7:40

There was a certain creditor which had two debtors: the one owed five hundred pence, and the other fifty.

41

And when they had nothing to pay, he frankly forgave them both. Tell me therefore, which of them will love him most?

42

Thou hast rightly judged.

43

Seest thou this woman? I entered into thine house, thou gavest me no water for my feet: but she hath washed my feet with tears, and wiped them with the hairs of her head.

44

Thou gavest me no kiss: but this woman since the time I came in hath not ceased to kiss my feet.    45

My head with oil thou didst not anoint: but this woman hath anointed my feet with ointment.    46

Wherefore I say unto thee, Her sins, which are many, are forgiven; for she loved much: but to whom little is forgiven, the same loveth little.    47

Thy sins are forgiven.    48

Thy faith hath saved thee; go in peace.    50

Jesus sends his disciples to prepare the Passover meal in Jerusalem.

Go into the city to such a man, and say unto him, The Master saith, My time is at hand; I will keep the passover at thy house with my disciples.    Mt 26:18

Go ye into the city, and there shall meet you a man bearing a pitcher of water: follow him.    Mk 14:13

And wheresoever he shall go in, say ye to the goodman of the house, The Master saith, Where is the guestchamber, where I shall eat the passover with my disciples?    14

And he will shew you a large upper room furnished and prepared: there make ready for us.    15

Go and prepare us the passover, that we may eat.

Lk 22: 8

Behold, when ye are entered into the city, there shall a man meet you, bearing a pitcher of water; follow him into the house where he entereth in.

10

And ye shall say unto the goodman of the house, The Master saith unto thee, Where is the guestchamber, where I shall eat the passover with my disciples?

11

And he shall shew you a large upper room furnished: there make ready.

12

Jesus partakes with his disciples of the Passover meal or the last supper and foresees that one of them will betray him.

Verily I say unto you, that one of you shall betray me.

Mt 26:21

He that dippeth his hand with me in the dish, the same shall betray me.

23

The Son of man goeth as it is written of him: but woe unto that man by whom the Son of man is betrayed! it had been good for that man if he had not been born.

24

Thou hast said.

25

Take, eat; this is my body.

26

Drink ye all of it;

27

For this is my blood of the new testament, which is shed for many for the remission of sins.

28

But I say unto you, I will not drink henceforth of this fruit of the vine, until that
day when I drink it new with you in my
Father's kingdom.

29

Verily I say unto you, One of you which
eateth with me shall betray me.

Mk14:18

It is one of the twelve, that dippeth with
me in the dish.

20

The Son of man indeed goeth, as it is
written of him: but woe to that man by
whom the Son of man is betrayed! good
were it for that man if he had never been
born.

21

Take, eat: this is my body.

22

This is my blood of the new testament,
which is shed for many.

24

Verily I say unto you, I will drink no more
of the fruit of the vine, until that day that
I drink it new in the kingdom of God.

25

With desire I have desired to eat this
passover with you before I suffer:

Lk 22:15

For I say unto you, I will not any more
eat thereof, until it be fulfilled in the kingdom of God.

16

Take this, and divide it among yourselves:

17

For I say unto you, I will not drink of the
fruit of the vine, until the kingdom of
God shall come.

18

This is my body which is given for you:
this do in remembrance of me.

19

This cup is the new testament in my blood, which is shed for you.

20

But, behold, the hand of him that betrayeth me is with me on the table.

21

And truly the Son of man goeth, as it was determined: but woe unto that man by whom he is betrayed!

22

Verily, verily, I say unto you, that one of you shall betray me.

Jn 13:21

He it is, to whom I shall give a sop, when I have dipped it.

26

That thou doest, do quickly.

27

After the meal Jesus washes his disciples' feet, interpreting the act as he performs it.

What I do thou knowest not now; but thou shalt know hereafter.

Jn 13: 7

If I wash thee not, thou hast no part with me.

8

He that is washed needeth not save to wash his feet, but is clean every whit: and ye are clean, but not all.

10

Know ye what I have done to you?

12

Ye call me Master and Lord: and ye say well; for so I am.

13

If I then, your Lord and Master, have washed your feet; ye also ought to wash one another's feet.

14

For I have given you an example, that ye
should do as I have done to you.                   15

Verily, verily, I say unto you, The servant       16
is not greater than his lord; neither he that
is sent greater than he that sent him.

If ye know these things, happy are ye if ye        17
do them.

I speak not of you all: I know whom I              18
have chosen: but that the scripture may
be fulfilled, He that eateth bread with me
hath lifted up his heel against me.

Now I tell you before it come, that, when          19
it is come to pass, ye may believe that I
am he.

Verily, verily, I say unto you, He that            20
receiveth whomsoever I send receiveth me;
and he that receiveth me receiveth him
that sent me.

He commands his
disciples to love
one another and,
having addressed
them for the last
time, prays for
them.

Now is the Son of man glorified, and God     Jn 13:31
is glorified in him.

If God be glorified in him, God shall also         32
glorify him in himself, and shall straightway glorify him.

Little children, yet a little while I am with       33
you. Ye shall seek me: and as I said unto
the Jews, Whither I go, ye cannot come;
so now I say to you.

A new commandment I give unto you, That ye love one another; as I have loved you, that ye also love one another.

34

By this shall all men know that ye are my disciples, if ye have love one to another.

35

Let not your heart be troubled: ye believe in God, believe also in me.

Jn 14: 1

In my Father's house are many mansions: if it were not so, I would have told you. I go to prepare a place for you.

2

And if I go and prepare a place for you, I will come again, and receive you unto myself; that where I am, there ye may be also.

3

And whither I go ye know, and the way ye know.

4

I am the way, the truth, and the life: no man cometh unto the Father, but by me.

6

If ye had known me, ye should have known my Father also: and from henceforth ye know him, and have seen him.

7

Have I been so long time with you, and yet hast thou not known me, Philip? he that hath seen me hath seen the Father; and how sayest thou then, Shew us the Father?

9

Believest thou not that I am in the Father, and the Father in me? the words that I speak unto you I speak not of myself: but the Father that dwelleth in me, he doeth the works.

10

Believe me that I am in the Father, and the Father in me: or else believe me for the very works' sake.   11

Verily, verily, I say unto you, He that believeth on me, the works that I do shall he do also; and greater works than these shall he do; because I go unto my Father.   12

And whatsoever ye shall ask in my name, that will I do, that the Father may be glorified in the Son.   13

If ye shall ask any thing in my name, I will do it.   14

If ye love me, keep my commandments.   15

And I will pray the Father, and he shall give you another Comforter, that he may abide with you for ever;   16

Even the Spirit of truth; whom the world cannot receive, because it seeth him not, neither knoweth him: but ye know him; for he dwelleth with you, and shall be in you.   17

I will not leave you comfortless: I will come to you.   18

Yet a little while, and the world seeth me no more; but ye see me: because I live, ye shall live also.   19

At that day ye shall know that I am in my Father, and ye in me, and I in you.   20

He that hath my commandments, and keepeth them, he it is that loveth me: and he that loveth me shall be loved of my Father, and I will love him, and will manifest myself to him.   21

If a man love me, he will keep my words: and my Father will love him, and we will come unto him, and make our abode with him. | 23

He that loveth me not keepeth not my sayings: and the word which ye hear is not mine, but the Father's which sent me. | 24

These things have I spoken unto you, being yet present with you. | 25

But the Comforter, which is the Holy Ghost, whom the Father will send in my name, he shall teach you all things, and bring all things to your remembrance, whatsoever I have said unto you. | 26

Peace I leave with you, my peace I give unto you: not as the world giveth, give I unto you. Let not your heart be troubled, neither let it be afraid. | 27

Ye have heard how I said unto you, I go away, and come again unto you. If ye loved me, ye would rejoice, because I said, I go unto the Father: for my Father is greater than I. | 28

And now I have told you before it come to pass, that, when it is come to pass, ye might believe. | 29

Hereafter I will not talk much with you: for the prince of this world cometh, and hath nothing in me. | 30

But that the world may know that I love the Father; and as the Father gave me commandment, even so I do. Arise, let us go hence. | 31

I am the true vine, and my Father is the husbandman.

Jn 15: 1

Every branch in me that beareth not fruit he taketh away: and every branch that beareth fruit, he purgeth it, that it may bring forth more fruit.

2

Now ye are clean through the word which I have spoken unto you.

3

Abide in me, and I in you. As the branch cannot bear fruit of itself, except it abide in the vine; no more can ye, except ye abide in me.

4

I am the vine, ye are the branches: He that abideth in me, and I in him, the same bringeth forth much fruit: for without me ye can do nothing.

5

If a man abide not in me, he is cast forth as a branch, and is withered; and men gather them, and cast them into the fire, and they are burned.

6

If ye abide in me, and my words abide in you, ye shall ask what ye will, and it shall be done unto you.

7

Herein is my Father glorified, that ye bear much fruit; so shall ye be my disciples.

8

As the Father hath loved me, so have I loved you: continue ye in my love.

9

If ye keep my commandments, ye shall abide in my love; even as I have kept my Father's commandments, and abide in his love.

10

These things have I spoken unto you, that my joy might remain in you, and that your joy might be full.

11

This is my commandment, That ye love one another, as I have loved you.

12

Greater love hath no man than this, that a man lay down his life for his friends.

13

Ye are my friends, if ye do whatsoever I command you.

14

Henceforth I call you not servants; for the servant knoweth not what his lord doeth: but I have called you friends; for all things that I have heard of my Father I have made known unto you.

15

Ye have not chosen me, but I have chosen you, and ordained you, that ye should go and bring forth fruit, and that your fruit should remain: that whatsoever ye shall ask of the Father in my name, he may give it you.

16

These things I command you, that ye love one another.

17

If the world hate you, ye know that it hated me before it hated you.

18

If ye were of the world, the world would love his own: but because ye are not of the world, but I have chosen you out of the world, therefore the world hateth you.

19

Remember the word that I said unto you, The servant is not greater than his lord. If they have persecuted me, they will also persecute you; if they have kept my saying, they will keep yours also.

20

But all these things will they do unto you for my name's sake, because they know not him that sent me. 21

If I had not come and spoken unto them, they had not had sin: but now they have no cloke for their sin. 22

He that hateth me hateth my Father also. 23

If I had not done among them the works which none other man did, they had not had sin: but now have they both seen and hated both me and my Father. 24

But this cometh to pass, that the word might be fulfilled that is written in their law, They hated me without a cause. 25

But when the Comforter is come, whom I will send unto you from the Father, even the Spirit of truth, which proceedeth from the Father, he shall testify of me: 26

And ye also shall bear witness, because ye have been with me from the beginning. 27

These things have I spoken unto you, that ye should not be offended. Jn 16: 1

They shall put you out of the synagogues: yea, the time cometh, that whosoever killeth you will think that he doeth God service. 2

And these things will they do unto you, because they have not known the Father, nor me. 3

But these things have I told you, that when the time shall come, ye may remem- 4 ber that I told you of them. And these things I said not unto you at the beginning, because I was with you.

But now I go my way to him that sent me; and none of you asketh me, Whither goest thou?    5

But because I have said these things unto you, sorrow hath filled your heart.    6

Nevertheless I tell you the truth; It is expedient for you that I go away: for if I go not away, the Comforter will not come unto you; but if I depart, I will send him unto you.    7

And when he is come, he will reprove the world of sin, and of righteousness, and of judgment:    8

Of sin, because they believe not on me;    9

Of righteousness, because I go to my Father, and ye see me no more;    10

Of judgment, because the prince of this world is judged.    11

I have yet many things to say unto you, but ye cannot bear them now.    12

Howbeit when he, the Spirit of truth, is come, he will guide you into all truth: for he shall not speak of himself; but whatsoever he shall hear, that shall he speak: and he will shew you things to come.    13

He shall glorify me: for he shall receive of mine, and shall shew it unto you.    14

All things that the Father hath are mine: therefore said I, that he shall take of mine, and shall shew it unto you.

15

A little while, and ye shall not see me: and again, a little while, and ye shall see me, because I go to the Father.

16

Do ye enquire among yourselves of that I said, A little while, and ye shall not see me: and again, a little while, and ye shall see me?

19

Verily, verily, I say unto you, That ye shall weep and lament, but the world shall rejoice: and ye shall be sorrowful, but your sorrow shall be turned into joy.

20

A woman when she is in travail hath sorrow, because her hour is come: but as soon as she is delivered of the child, she remembereth no more the anguish, for joy that a man is born into the world.

21

And ye now therefore have sorrow: but I will see you again, and your heart shall rejoice, and your joy no man taketh from you.

22

And in that day ye shall ask me nothing. Verily, verily, I say unto you, Whatsoever ye shall ask the Father in my name, he will give it you.

23

Hitherto have ye asked nothing in my name: ask, and ye shall receive, that your joy may be full.

24

These things have I spoken unto you in proverbs: but the time cometh, when I

25

shall no more speak unto you in proverbs, but I shall shew you plainly of the
Father.

At that day ye shall ask in my name: and
I say not unto you, that I will pray the
Father for you:

For the Father himself loveth you, because
ye have loved me, and have believed that
I came out from God.

I came forth from the Father, and am
come into the world: again, I leave the
world, and go to the Father.

Do ye now believe?

Behold, the hour cometh, yea, is now
come, that ye shall be scattered, every man
to his own, and shall leave me alone: and
yet I am not alone, because the Father is
with me.

These things I have spoken unto you, that
in me ye might have peace. In the world
ye shall have tribulation: but be of good
cheer; I have overcome the world.

Father, the hour is come; glorify thy Son,
that thy Son also may glorify thee:

As thou hast given him power over all
flesh, that he should give eternal life to as
many as thou hast given him.

And this is life eternal, that they might
know thee the only true God, and Jesus
Christ, whom thou hast sent.

I have glorified thee on the earth: I have finished the work which thou gavest me to do.

4

And now, O Father, glorify thou me with thine own self with the glory which I had with thee before the world was.

5

I have manifested thy name unto the men which thou gavest me out of the world: thine they were, and thou gavest them me; and they have kept thy word.

6

Now they have known that all things whatsoever thou hast given me are of thee.

7

For I have given unto them the words which thou gavest me; and they have received them, and have known surely that I came out from thee, and they have believed that thou didst send me.

8

I pray for them: I pray not for the world, but for them which thou hast given me; for they are thine.

9

And all mine are thine, and thine are mine; and I am glorified in them.

10

And now I am no more in the world, but these are in the world, and I come to thee. Holy Father, keep through thine own name those whom thou hast given me, that they may be one, as we are.

11

While I was with them in the world, I kept them in thy name: those that thou gavest me I have kept, and none of them is lost, but the son of perdition; that the scripture might be fulfilled.

12

And now come I to thee; and these things I speak in the world, that they might have my joy fulfilled in themselves. 13

I have given them thy word; and the world hath hated them, because they are not of the world, even as I am not of the world. 14

I pray not that thou shouldest take them out of the world, but that thou shouldest keep them from the evil. 15

They are not of the world, even as I am not of the world. 16

Sanctify them through thy truth: thy word is truth. 17

As thou hast sent me into the world, even so have I also sent them into the world. 18

And for their sakes I sanctify myself, that they also might be sanctified through the truth. 19

Neither pray I for these alone, but for them also which shall believe on me through their word; 20

That they all may be one; as thou, Father, art in me, and I in thee, that they also may be one in us: that the world may believe that thou hast sent me. 21

And the glory which thou gavest me I have given them; that they may be one, even as we are one: 22

I in them, and thou in me, that they may be made perfect in one; and that the world may know that thou hast sent me, and hast loved them, as thou hast loved me. 23

Father, I will that they also, whom thou hast given me, be with me where I am; that they may behold my glory, which thou hast given me: for thou lovedst me before the foundation of the world.

24

O righteous Father, the world hath not known thee: but I have known thee, and these have known that thou hast sent me.

25

And I have declared unto them thy name, and will declare it: that the love wherewith thou hast loved me may be in them, and I in them.

26

Jesus goes with his disciples to the Mount of Olives, where he foresees that Peter will deny him.

All ye shall be offended because of me this night: for it is written, I will smite the shepherd, and the sheep of the flock shall be scattered abroad.

Mt 26:31

But after I am risen again, I will go before you into Galilee.

32

Verily I say unto thee, That this night, before the cock crow, thou shalt deny me thrice.

34

All ye shall be offended because of me this night: for it is written, I will smite the shepherd, and the sheep shall be scattered.

Mk 14:27

But after that I am risen, I will go before you into Galilee.

28

Verily I say unto thee, That this day, even in this night, before the cock crow twice, thou shalt deny me thrice.

30

### Related Sayings

Simon, Simon, behold, Satan hath desired to have you, that he may sift you as wheat:

Lk 22:31

But I have prayed for thee, that thy faith fail not: and when thou art converted, strengthen thy brethren.

32

I tell thee, Peter, the cock shall not crow this day, before that thou shalt thrice deny that thou knowest me.

34

When I sent you without purse, and scrip, and shoes, lacked ye any thing?

35

But now, he that hath a purse, let him take it, and likewise his scrip: and he that hath no sword, let him sell his garment, and buy one.

36

For I say unto you, that this that is written must yet be accomplished in me, And he was reckoned among the transgressors: for the things concerning me have an end.

37

It is enough.

38

Whither I go, thou canst not follow me now; but thou shalt follow me afterwards.

Jn 13:36

Wilt thou lay down thy life for my sake? Verily, verily, I say unto thee, The cock shall not crow, till thou hast denied me thrice.

38

He suffers in the Garden of Gethsemane while his disciples sleep.

Sit ye here, while I go and pray yonder.

Mt 26:36

My soul is exceeding sorrowful, even unto death: tarry ye here, and watch with me.

38

O my Father, if it be possible, let this cup pass from me: nevertheless not as I will, but as thou wilt.

39

What, could ye not watch with me one hour?

40

Watch and pray, that ye enter not into temptation: the spirit indeed is willing, but the flesh is weak.

41

O my Father, if this cup may not pass away from me, except I drink it, thy will be done.

42

Sleep on now, and take your rest: behold, the hour is at hand, and the Son of man is betrayed into the hands of sinners.

45

Rise, let us be going: behold, he is at hand that doth betray me.

46

Sit ye here, while I shall pray.

Mk 14:32

My soul is exceeding sorrowful unto death: tarry ye here, and watch.

34

Abba, Father, all things are possible unto thee; take away this cup from me: nevertheless not what I will, but what thou wilt.

36

Simon, sleepest thou? couldest not thou watch one hour?

37

| | |
|---|---|
| Watch ye and pray, lest ye enter into temptation. The spirit truly is ready, but the flesh is weak. | 38 |
| Sleep on now, and take your rest: it is enough, the hour is come; behold, the Son of man is betrayed into the hands of sinners. | 41 |
| Rise up, let us go; lo, he that betrayeth me is at hand. | 42 |
| Pray that ye enter not into temptation. | Lk 22:40 |
| Father, if thou be willing, remove this cup from me: nevertheless not my will, but thine, be done. | 42 |
| Why sleep ye? rise and pray, lest ye enter into temptation. | 46 |

Judas Iscariot betrays Jesus to a body of armed men under orders from the High Priest.

| | |
|---|---|
| Friend, wherefore art thou come? | Mt 26:50 |
| Put up again thy sword into his place: for all they that take the sword shall perish with the sword. | 52 |
| Thinkest thou that I cannot now pray to my Father, and he shall presently give me more than twelve legions of angels? | 53 |
| But how then shall the scriptures be fulfilled, that thus it must be? | 54 |

Are ye come out as against a thief with swords and staves for to take me? I sat daily with you teaching in the temple, and ye laid no hold on me.                                                  55

But all this was done, that the scriptures of the prophets might be fulfilled.          56


Are ye come out, as against a thief, with swords and with staves to take me?          Mk14:48

I was daily with you in the temple teaching, and ye took me not: but the scriptures must be fulfilled.                                49


Judas, betrayest thou the Son of man with a kiss?                                         Lk 22:48

Suffer ye thus far.                                      51

Be ye come out, as against a thief, with swords and staves?                               52

When I was daily with you in the temple, ye stretched forth no hands against me: but this is your hour, and the power of darkness.                                             53


Whom seek ye?                                           Jn 18: 4

I am he.                                                 5

Whom seek ye?                                           7

I have told you that I am he: if therefore ye seek me, let these go their way.          8

Put up thy sword into the sheath: the cup which my Father hath given me, shall I not drink it?                                          11

Jesus is led before
Annas, father-in-law
to the High Priest
Caiaphas.

I spake openly to the world; I ever taught in the synagogue, and in the temple, whither the Jews always resort; and in secret have I said nothing.

Jn 18:20

Why askest thou me? ask them which heard me, what I have said unto them: behold, they know what I said.

21

If I have spoken evil, bear witness of the evil: but if well, why smitest thou me?

23

Jesus is led before
Caiaphas, who
asks whether he be
the Christ.

Thou hast said: nevertheless I say unto you, Hereafter shall ye see the Son of man sitting on the right hand of power, and coming in the clouds of heaven.

Mt 26:64

I am: and ye shall see the Son of man sitting on the right hand of power, and coming in the clouds of heaven.

Mk14:62

He is tried before
the Sanhedrin,
whose members repeat Caiaphas's
question.

If I tell you, ye will not believe:

Lk 22:67

And if I also ask you, ye will not answer me, nor let me go.

68

Hereafter shall the Son of man sit on the right hand of the power of God.                    69

Ye say that I am.                                            70

The Sanhedrin delivers Jesus to Pontius Pilate, the Roman Governor, who asks whether he be the King of the Jews.

Thou sayest.                                               Mt 27: 11

Thou sayest it.                                             Mk15: 2

Thou sayest it.                                             Lk 23: 3

Sayest thou this thing of thyself, or did others tell it thee of me?                          Jn 18: 34

My kingdom is not of this world: if my kingdom were of this world, then would my servants fight, that I should not be delivered to the Jews: but now is my kingdom not from hence.                              36

Thou sayest that I am a king. To this end was I born, and for this cause came I into the world, that I should bear witness unto the truth. Every one that is of the truth heareth my voice.                            37

Pontius Pilate hesitates before delivering him to be crucified at Golgotha.

Thou couldest have no power at all against me, except it were given thee from above:           Jn 19: 11

therefore he that delivered me unto thee hath the greater sin.

Jesus responds to a company of women who bewail and lament him on the way to the cross.

Lk 23:28

Daughters of Jerusalem, weep not for me, but weep for yourselves, and for your children.

For, behold, the days are coming, in the which they shall say, Blessed are the barren, and the wombs that never bare, and the paps which never gave suck.

29

Then shall they begin to say to the mountains, Fall on us; and to the hills, Cover us.

30

For if they do these things in a green tree, what shall be done in the dry?

31

He prays at Golgotha for those who crucify him.

Lk 23:34

Father, forgive them; for they know not what they do.

He responds to a criminal crucified beside him.

Lk 23:43

Verily I say unto thee, To day shalt thou be with me in paradise.

He entrusts his
mother to the care
of John.

Woman, behold thy son!

Jn 19:26

Behold thy mother!

27

He cries out to God
in agony.

Eli, Eli, lama sabachthani? *that is to say,*
*My God, my God, why hast thou forsaken*
*me?*

Mt 27:46

Eloi, Eloi, lama sabachthani? *which is,*
*being interpreted, My God, my God, why*
*hast thou forsaken me?*

Mk15:34

Having drunk vin-
egar from a
sponge, he fulfills
the scriptures.

I thirst.

Jn 19:28

It is finished:

30

He dies on the
cross.

Father, into thy hands I commend my
spirit:

Lk 23:46

Jesus surprises
Mary Magdalene at
his tomb.

Woman, why weepest thou? whom seekest
thou?

Jn 20:15

Mary.

16

Touch me not; for I am not yet ascended to my Father: but go to my brethren, and say unto them, I ascend unto my Father, and your Father; and to my God, and your God.

17

He meets Mary Magdalene and another Mary on their way to tell the disciples he is risen.

All hail.

Mt 28: 9

Be not afraid: go tell my brethren that they go into Galilee, and there shall they see me.

10

He shows himself to ten of the eleven (Thomas excepted) in Jerusalem.

Peace be unto you.

Jn 20:19

Peace be unto you: as my Father hath sent me, even so send I you.

21

Receive ye the Holy Ghost:

22

Whose soever sins ye remit, they are remitted unto them; and whose soever sins ye retain, they are retained.

23

He expounds the scriptures to two disciples on the road to Emmaus where, still unrecognized, he sits down to break bread with them.

What manner of communications are these that ye have one to another, as ye walk, and are sad?

Lk 24:16

| | |
|---|---|
| What things? | 19 |
| O fools, and slow of heart to believe all that the prophets have spoken: | 25 |
| Ought not Christ to have suffered these things, and to enter into his glory? | 26 |

He shows himself to the assembled disciples (Thomas included) in Jerusalem, resolving all doubt that he is flesh and blood.

| | |
|---|---|
| Peace be unto you. | Lk 24:36 |
| Why are ye troubled? and why do thoughts arise in your hearts? | 38 |
| Behold my hands and my feet, that it is I myself: handle me, and see; for a spirit hath not flesh and bones, as ye see me have. | 39 |
| Have ye here any meat? | 41 |

*Related Saying*

| | |
|---|---|
| Peace be unto you. | Jn 20:26 |
| Reach hither thy finger, and behold my hands; and reach hither thy hand, and thrust it into my side: and be not faithless, but believing. | 27 |
| Thomas, because thou hast seen me, thou hast believed: blessed are they that have not seen, and yet have believed. | 29 |

He calls seven dis-
ciples on the Sea of
Galilee to bring their
catch and dine with
him.

Children, have ye any meat?

Jn 21: 5

Cast the net on the right side of the ship, and ye shall find.

6

Bring of the fish which ye have now caught.

10

Come and dine.

12

Simon, son of Jonas, lovest thou me more than these? Feed my lambs.

15

Simon, son of Jonas, lovest thou me? Feed my sheep.

16

Simon, son of Jonas, lovest thou me? Feed my sheep.

17

Verily, verily, I say unto thee, When thou wast young, thou girdedst thyself, and walkedst whither thou wouldest: but when thou shalt be old, thou shalt stretch forth thy hands, and another shall gird thee, and carry thee whither thou wouldest not.

18

Follow me.

19

If I will that he tarry till I come, what is that to thee? follow thou me.

22

He exhorts the eleven
disciples on a moun-
tain in Galilee to bap-
tize all nations.

All power is given unto me in heaven and in earth.

Mt 28: 18

Go ye therefore, and teach all nations, baptizing them in the name of the Father, and of the Son, and of the Holy Ghost:

19

Teaching them to observe all things whatsoever I have commanded you: and, lo, I am with you alway, even unto the end of the world.

20

He urges the eleven disciples in Galilee to preach the gospel to all creation.

Go ye into all the world, and preach the gospel to every creature.

Mk16:15

He that believeth and is baptized shall be saved; but he that believeth not shall be damned.

16

And these signs shall follow them that believe; In my name shall they cast out devils; they shall speak with new tongues;

17

They shall take up serpents; and if they drink any deadly thing, it shall not hurt them; they shall lay hands on the sick, and they shall recover.

18

*Related Saying*

I beheld Satan as lightning fall from heaven.

Lk 10:18

Behold, I give unto you power to tread on serpents and scorpions, and over all the power of the enemy: and nothing shall by any means hurt you.

19

Notwithstanding in this rejoice not, that the spirits are subject unto you; but rather rejoice, because your names are written in heaven.

20

He expounds the scriptures to the assembled disciples in Jerusalem, telling them how to act but bidding them first wait to receive power from God.

These are the words which I spake unto you, while I was yet with you, that all things must be fulfilled, which were written in the law of Moses, and in the prophets, and in the psalms, concerning me.

Lk 24:44

Thus it is written, and thus it behoved Christ to suffer, and to rise from the dead the third day:

46

And that repentance and remission of sins should be preached in his name among all nations, beginning at Jerusalem.

47

And ye are witnesses of these things.

48

And, behold, I send the promise of my Father upon you: but tarry ye in the city of Jerusalem, until ye be endued with power from on high.

49

*Related Saying*

[B]ut wait for the promise of the Father, which ye have heard of me.

Ac 1: 4

For John truly baptized with water; but
ye shall be baptized with the Holy Ghost
not many days hence.

5

It is not for you to know the times or the
seasons, which the Father hath put in his
own power.

7

But ye shall receive power, after that the
Holy Ghost is come upon you: and ye
shall be witnesses unto me both in Jerusalem, and in all Judaea, and in Samaria,
and unto the uttermost part of the earth.

8